A New Conversation with Men

Coach Michael Taylor

What people are saying about

A New Conversation With Men

"This is far more than a "self-help" book, this is a guide to actually living the life you may have only dreamt of, having the real happiness you've always needed and deserved, but never had. For those ready for something new and different, a happier and fulfilling life, but not knowing where to turn, look no further than Michael Taylor's exceptional guide, "A New Conversation With Men." Not just for men, this book is for anyone wanting to live a happier life. My highest recommendation."

– CoyotePrimeBlogger
(http://coyoteprime-runningcauseicantfly.blogspot.com/)

A New Conversation with Men is one of the most unique books I have ever read in my 16 years of reviewing books on gender and masculinity. Taylor's commitment to making the universe a better place is truly admirable.

– J. Steven Svoboda (http://mensightmagazine.com/)

"I think Michael Taylor's message is very current, important, and much in need today. If we can just get a few more men to hear his

message, and ask them to pass it on, pay it forward and walk the talk, maybe just maybe we can reach some of those lost men, brothers and sons". "This book is a fantastic read, open and honest talk. I strongly recommend people "Gift" this book to a male they love."

– Debra Owsley (www.simplysaidreadingaccessories.blogspot.com)

A must-read not just for men

Although it is geared towards men, there are a few chapters that I found very useful. The chapters on Joy, Passion and Creativity, Spirituality and What's Love Got to Do With It are great, my favorite is Transformation."

"I will definitely go back and read this book again. Highly recommended!"

– Jacque Cartwright Book reviewer (readerspoils.com)

Silence is Not a Virtue

Wow, this was fabulous. Michael did not make this read boring or difficult. He wrote with truth and feelings and his words brought shivers to my bones. His story reminded me of many men that I have met throughout my life and also made me think of myself.

I loved this book and have already told others about it. I am waiting for my husband to read it so he can feel better about the road his life has taken but, at the same instance, he can realize that the road can turn.

Kudos Michael Taylor! This is a MUST-READ.

– Lionpro "Deborah" Book reviewer (www.readerspoils.com)

This book is destined to start a revolution in how men see themselves
A New Conversation with Men teaches men how to change without sacrificing their personal success and their masculinity and, in doing so, reclaim their joy. From an unbiased viewpoint, I would say that this book is destined to start a revolution in how men see themselves and their role in society. As a woman, I would like to say that this is the book we've been waiting to hit the market for centuries!

– Heather Shockney Book reviewer (www.readerspoils.com)

Finally! A book that makes you feel proud to be a man and challenges you to become a better one.

– J. Covington – (customer testimonial)

A New Conversation with Men explains why it is OK for men to be open and honest about the feelings they have. Each chapter of the book will teach men how they can have a better relationship with their self, and the other people in their lives. I recommend this book to all men. Even if they think they know everything it takes to be a "real" man, they will benefit from reading this book.

– Renee Malove Book reviewer (www.readerspoils.com)

I know a lot of men will be hesitant to read a book like this (I know I was) but I must admit it is one of the most thought-provoking books I've ever read. It really challenged me to question what it means to be a man and it shattered some of my long-held beliefs about manhood. To be completely honest, I'm a much better man as a result of reading this book.

– Samuel J. Gibson (customer testimonial)

Whenever I finish reviewing a book, I usually put it on a special shelf on my bookcase, where it sits indefinitely without being touched; a sort of book reviewer's game trophy. Not so with "A New Conversation with Men" by Michael Taylor. As I am writing this, the book is sitting on my desk within arm's reach, and there it will sit for the foreseeable future. I intend to read it again, slowly, and then a few times more. Who knows, I might be the next person to join the revolution. It certainly can't hurt. It will make me a better man, and perhaps make the world a better place in which to live. Attention all men: read this book before it is too late!

– Ron Standerfer book reviewer (www.readerviews.com)

A New Conversation with Men

Coach Michael Taylor

© 2011 by Michael Taylor
Published by Creation Publishing Group LLC 1219 Nikki Lane,
Stafford, Texas 77477 www.creationpublishing.com

ISBN: 978-0-9641894-2-3

Library of Congress Control Number: 2011917722

Printed in the United States of America Second printing
All rights reserved. No part of this book may be reproduced, stored in a retrieval system or transmitted in any form or by any means without the prior written permission of the publishers, except by a reviewer who may quote brief passages in a review to be printed in a newspaper, magazine or journal.

Acknowledgments

To my Creator:

There are no words that come close to expressing the gratitude I feel in my heart. I am so grateful for all the lessons and life experiences You placed in front of me to help me discover who I really am. I see Your purpose for my life, and every piece of my life's puzzle fits perfectly into Your divine plan. Thank You for the gifts and for the recognition that I'm supposed to use them in Your service. I surrender to Your divine plan and commit my life to be in service to You. I love You more than love!

To my wife Bedra:

For the past eight years or so, I have been telling you that I would live my dreams, and we would have an amazing life together. The beautiful part about our relationship is that our love for each other is unconditional and not based on "stuff." You have loved me unconditionally and supported me in every way imaginable. I really appreciate you for all you have done. You have been the absolute perfect wife for me, and I have always known that we would live happily ever after. The sky is the limit for us. As I have always told you, you've already won the lottery! The best is yet to come. I love you!

ACKNOWLEDGMENTS

To my SoulCircle friends, Robin, Tom, Tim, Jackie, Jan, Bonnie, Jack and Nancy:

You guys have supported and challenged me for the past 8 years to become the grandest version of the greatest vision I have for myself. As a result of my participation in the Circle, I have created a deep sense of authenticity and a connection to my source that defies description. Thank you for your openness and willingness to speak from the heart. I am a much better man because of your love and support.

To my mom:

Your baby boy promised you he would live his dreams. I'm so glad to have a mom like you who instilled a positive attitude and excellent work ethic in me at a very young age. You are always with me. I love you!

To my kids, Charles, Mike, and Katrina:

Nothing makes me prouder than being able to say that I have been a great dad. I've made my share of mistakes, but I never let anything get in the way of staying connected to each of you. Watching you guys grow up and become successful independent individuals makes my heart sing. I am extremely proud of each one of you. I love you all.

To my sisters, Lela and Shirl:

Although we may not communicate that often, I really appreciate the fact that you both really believe in me. Know that I love you both and wish you the best. Shirl, I'll be sure to send you a shout-out when I get on Oprah. Roy and Sherman, I love you, too!

To a very special group of men, Gene M., Judge M., Ernest P., Jonathan O., Russell R., Arthur J., Kenny B., and Charles M.:

Each of you men epitomizes what true masculinity really is. Thank you for the stimulating and challenging conversations. Our dialogs have definitely been part of the inspiration for this book. Keep growing and keep expanding your awareness.

— Michael "Happy Ass" Taylor

Contents

Introduction 1

Chapter One: How the Conversation Began 5

Chapter Two: Our Greatest Challenge 31

Chapter Three: The Five Illusions of Manhood 55

Chapter Four: The Five Masks of Masculinity 69

Chapter Five: Transformation 89

Chapter Six: What's Love Got to Do with It? 121

Chapter Seven: Fatherlessness 145

Chapter Eight: Joy, Passion, and Creativity 167

Chapter Nine: Spirituality 185

Chapter Ten: The Revolution 211

About the author 222

Introduction

It is my fervent belief that men are frustrated, tired and hungry. They are frustrated because they are trapped in an old paradigm that no longer works. They are frustrated because they are searching for new and better ways to exist as a man yet they have failed in this search. They don't know where to turn, and they are becoming desperate for a new way of being and relating as a man.

They are tired of watching their families fall apart, their health deteriorate, and their wallets be emptied by divorce, materialism, and senseless addictions that rob them of not only their money but their self-esteem and dignity as well. They are tired of working at jobs that they hate just to try to keep up with the Joneses. They are tired of the emptiness and feeling of meaninglessness in their soul that tells them that there has to be another way to exist, yet they don't know how to change.

They are hungry for something new and different, and I believe that something different is *A New Conversation with Men*.

I know this because I used to be one of those men. I know what it's like to be frustrated, tired, and hungry, and for the last twenty years, I have been removing this frustration, eliminating my exhaustion, and satisfying my hunger to become a better man. As a result, I will admit that my life is now working, and I feel happy and blessed to be a man.

INTRODUCTION

I wanted to share my story in hopes of empowering you to follow in my footsteps. I simply want you to become a better man.

This book is written to assist any man who wants to do just that: be-come a better man. It is written for the man who is sick and tired of being sick and tired, and it is written for that courageous man who refuses to settle for mediocrity and wants to live a life of excellence.

It's been said that "There is no power in the universe that can stop an idea whose time has come." I believe the time has come for *A New Conversation with Men,* and nothing can stop it. This book is written to start a new revolution for the hearts, minds and souls of men everywhere, and my hope is that this revolution changes the world for the better.

"Our deepest fear is not that we are inadequate. Our deepest fear is that we are powerful beyond measure."

— Marianne Williamson

Chapter One

How the Conversation Began

The intention of this book is simple: I want to create a new paradigm of masculinity in this country. What I mean by that is that I want men to recognize that some of the old ways of being a man in society no longer work. What is needed are some new ways of being a man that empowers men to become better husbands, fathers, lovers, and friends. In this new paradigm, men will learn to embrace new roles as men, which I believe will help eradicate some of the social issues that currently plague our society. These issues include (but are not limited to) divorce, poverty, domestic violence, drug addiction, and fatherlessness. In my opinion, these are the greatest challenges facing our country today.

I must admit that I am not an expert in this endeavor. I do not hold any formal degrees, and I definitely do not claim to have all the answers. Al-though I do not have any academic titles, what I do have is a strong conviction to share some of the lessons and principles I have learned that have helped me become a better man. My hope is that in sharing these lessons I can empower you to become a better man also. Once that happens, you can join me in creating this new paradigm of masculinity I'm writing about. As you read through this book, try to imagine that you are listening to a trusted friend. I can assure you that my motives are pure, and I am definitely on your team. I want nothing more than to empower you to reach your full potential. Know that there will be things that I say that you may disagree with. At the same time, there will be things that you may totally agree with. The key is to keep an open mind and listen to that still-small voice of wisdom within you. Trust your inner voice as you read the contents of this book. Know that if you feel any discomfort as you read, it probably means that you are learning some valuable lessons. Discomfort is a sure sign of growth, and that should be the reason you are reading this book. There is a wonderful saying, "If you're not growing, you're dying."

Be committed to growing, and keep an open mind.

To sum it up, my intention is to start a revolution; not a revolution of physical force or control but a revolution of the hearts, minds and spirits of men. This is an inner revolution whose time has come. I welcome you to the revolution.

So are you ready? Are you ready to engage in a new conversation with men? Are you ready to join me in creating a new paradigm of masculinity? I believe the answer is yes, so let's begin at the beginning. This is how the conversation began.

When I was nine or ten years old, I remember sitting down having a conversation with my grandfather. I remember telling him that one day I was going to be rich. When asked how I planned on becoming rich, I replied by stating that one day, I would own my own company, and that I would be a very successful entrepreneur.

Not only do I remember the conversation, I also remember the very strong conviction I felt when I made the comment. There was a part of me that intuitively knew that this was my destiny, and I was put on this planet to lead an extraordinary life. No matter what it took, I was committed to making this happen.

At the age of thirteen, I actually started my first company. It was a janitorial company in which I would go to different companies and clean up for them. It began when I was walking home from school one day and happened to overhear an argument between an employer and one of his employees at a local motorcycle shop. The employee was cursing and screaming, saying that it was not his job to sweep and clean up, and he was threatening to walk out if the owner did not get someone else to do the dirty work. I sensed an opportunity and walked up to the owner and told him I had overheard the conversation. I told him that I was willing to clean up for him if he would give me a job. The owner looked at me with a smile and asked how much I would charge for my services. I had no idea how much money to ask for so I asked him what did he think my services were worth. He put his arm on my shoulder and said he would make me a deal. He suggested that I go ahead and clean up his garage and after I was finished, he would determine what my services were worth.

That seemed fair enough, so I began my task. I knew this was a golden opportunity for me, and I knew that I needed to do my best. Fortunately, my mother had instilled a very strong work ethic in me, and I cleaned that garage as if I was going to receive a million dollars. It was absolutely spotless when I finished. I did such a great job that the guy that was cursing about having to clean up walked over to the owner and told him that he needed to hire me right then and now. The owner agreed, and I landed my first job. Our agreement was that he would give me five dollars each time I cleaned the garage. It took me approximately thirty minutes to complete my task, so in essence, I was making ten dollars an hour. The minimum wage at the time was a dollar and sixty-five cents an hour. This was like hitting the lottery to me. The good news was that the owner had a few friends that also owned garages, and I ended up having three or four different customers as a result of his referrals. My very first company was born. I was an entrepreneur even though I really did not know what that meant at the time. This was my first taste of capitalism and success, and I loved it. The company lasted approximately two years, and then I moved on to other endeavors.

In high school, I really struggled with making decent grades. It's not that I wasn't smart; I was actually just bored. I had had a taste of entrepreneurship, and I could not see the correlation between getting a high school diploma and becoming rich. There was something in me that was pulling me to my ultimate destiny. I wanted to be successful, and I wanted it now!

During this time, I was enrolled in a special program that allowed me to go to school half a day and then go to work. I did not participate in sports because I believed that the way to live my dreams was by owning my own company, so I invested every minute I could into learning about the business world. Going to work was exciting and exhilarating. I would sit down and speak with managers and ask them questions about climbing the corporate ladder. I devoured books on management, motivation and finance. Reading and studying about business was a lot different from what I was being taught in school. As I read business books, I was filled with a passion for learning, while in school, I was unmotivated and bored.

By the age of seventeen, I was attending seminars and lectures about getting rich and living the American dream. One significant event I attended was a motivational seminar put on by a vacuum cleaner manufacturer. I remember being mesmerized by the speaker. He had this amazing energy about him, and he was captivating and intelligent. His passion was infectious, and I seemed to fall into a trance as I listened to him tell the story of how he became a millionaire selling vacuum cleaners.

As I listened to his story, I began to believe that I could do the same thing. As he spoke, all I could see were dollar signs and the huge mansion that I had dreamed about since I was a young boy. Was this the opportunity that I had been searching for? Was this my path to riches and fame? At the end of the seminar, the presenter said two things that made me believe that I had found my destiny. Number one, he said that I did not need a college education or a high-school diploma to become rich. Number two, he said that all I needed was a positive attitude and a willingness to work harder than anyone else, and I would succeed.

I knew in my heart that I was willing to work hard and maintain a positive attitude. I also believed that I was smart enough to learn whatever was necessary to become a success. I then decided that I needed to seize this opportunity and not wait another moment to begin fulfilling my dream. I made the mistake of deciding to drop out of high school to pursue my dream of becoming rich. Of course, my mother was extremely disappointed in my decision. She did everything she possibly could to talk me out of it, but my mind was made up. I dropped out of school and began my journey to wealth and success.

So there I was: young, motivated, ambitious, and ready to take on the world. Although my mother disagreed with my decision, she still supported and encouraged me to do my best. She told me to work hard and do whatever it took to reach my goals. As always, she loved and encouraged me even though she disagreed with me.

Have you ever noticed how mothers are usually right about major life- changing decisions? This time was no different. My mother was right. I had definitely made the wrong decision. After several months and over three hundred cold calls, I never sold a single vacuum cleaner.

I was disappointed and dejected, but I still did not let go of my dream. I had to make some decisions about my future, and I needed to find a way to get back on track. The first decision I needed to make was whether I would return to school. Although I knew it was the right decision, there was a part of me that simply did not believe that a high-school education was important. I felt very strongly that if I really applied myself to learning about business, I would ultimately achieve my goals. I told my mom that I wanted to pursue a full-time job instead of going back to school.

Once again, my mom told me that I was making the wrong decision. She assured me that a high-school diploma was the first step in achieving my dreams, and I needed to secure my diploma before I did anything else. I assured her that one day, I would receive my diploma, but the time wasn't right. I wanted to break into the business world, and now was the time for me to do it. As she had done before, my mom encouraged me to get focused and make my dreams become a reality. Although she disagreed with my decision, she provided me with support and encouragement. I assured her that I knew what I was doing, and that I would not disappoint her. As a matter of fact, not disappointing her was the main reason that I wanted to be a success. I knew that eventually, I would make her proud, and once I became rich, I would be able to give her all the things she deserved.

My journey to my destiny had begun. The first thing I needed to do was to find a job and start building my future. What I hadn't anticipated was the fact that most companies aren't interested in hiring a high- school dropout. Although I knew that I was a fast learner, had a positive mental attitude, and was very dependable, I had an extremely difficult time simply getting an opportunity to showcase my skills. Every company wanted at least a high-school diploma before I could even fill out an application.

After a few months, I began to rethink my decision. I had no success in locating a job, and I knew that I was disappointing my mom, and most importantly, myself. Maybe I should go back to school to get my diploma and then pursue my dream. Maybe I was just dreaming and needed to come back to reality and follow the status quo.

Although I had some doubts, I knew that I could not go along with the status quo. I intuitively knew that I could not give up on my dream, and no matter what it took, I had to persevere and make it happen. During this time, I maintained my commitment to personal growth and development. I had continued reading motivational books and stories of people who had overcome great obstacles to live their dreams. These books helped me keep a positive attitude and kept the fire burning within me. As I read their stories, I felt a strong sense that I, too, would one day overcome all of the challenges placed before me. I knew that one day, I would be sharing my story of overcoming seemingly insurmountable obstacles and that my story would motivate others the way their stories had motivated me.

HOW THE CONVERSATION BEGAN

I instinctively knew that one day, my big break was going to come, and all I had to do was to keep moving confidently in the direction of my dreams. I became more determined than ever. To make sure that I would secure a job, I decided that I needed to call on at least five potential jobs or fill out at least five applications a day. Every day, I would take the daily newspaper and begin my search. I would make phone calls and set up interviews. I would make cold calls to companies that posted help-wanted signs. I was a man on a mission, and I refused to quit. After approximately five months, I began to feel as if my big break was just around the corner. Because of all the effort I had put into finding a job, I had become much more confident and comfortable with the whole interviewing process. It was as if I were practicing for my upcoming big break, and the preceding months were simply preparing me for my ultimate destiny.

After approximately six months, my big break finally arrived. I was going through the help-wanted section and I ran across an ad that said, "Major building-supply retailer looking for salesmen. Starting salary 800 dollars a month plus commission." I remember reading that ad and then calculating to see if I would be able to move out and get my own apartment with that salary. Although I had not even gone for an interview or filled out an application, I begin acting as if I already had the job. I actually convinced myself that it was mine, and I was already making plans for building my future. I was excited because I somehow knew that I was going to get that job.

When I arrived at the company's location, all sorts of thoughts were going through my mind. Be articulate, listen attentively, don't talk too much, be polite, be assertive, be confident. These were all things that I had learned through reading business and management books. The time had come for me to put into practice all of these valuable business lessons.

Although I had committed all of these tips to memory, I still could not repress who I was and my personality. I have always been an extraverted optimistic type, and by some people's definition, "a little cocky." So I wasn't surprised at all by my initial approach. I walked into the store and asked for the manager. Unfortunately, he was not available, so I had to speak with his assistant. As his assistant walked up to me, I extended a very firm and confident handshake, something else I learned from the business books. I looked him squarely in the eye and began the conversation, something like this. "Hi, my name is Michael Taylor. Did you know that today is our lucky day? The reason I know this is because today, I am going to save you some money and at the same time, I am going to make some money. Don't you think that is a lucky day for both of us?"

The poor guy didn't know how to respond. He had that deer-in-the- headlights sort of look and he finally ask me what I meant.

So I responded, "Well, you see, I saw your ad in the paper today. And now, you can take the ad out of the paper, which will save you a lot of money, and you can give me the job, which will make me some money. Don't you think that's a win-win situation for both of us? All of the business books teach you about creating win-win situations. I was so glad I paid attention.

The guy looked at me with a smile and told me that he obviously did not have the authority to take the ad out of the paper, but he did want me to fill out an application. As I began filling out the application, I remembered another lesson I learned from the business books. That lesson was to always leave a positive impression. So after I completed the application, I asked the assistant if he had a few moments just to tell me a little bit about the company and the position. I then took it a step further and began asking him about how long he had been with the company and what he liked and disliked about working there. After approximately thirty minutes, I knew his wife's name, how many kids he had, what he liked to drink, and who his favorite sports team was. We were talking as though we were old friends. I had definitely created a positive impression that I knew would pay off.

He then informed me that the manager would not be back for several days, and he would contact me as soon as the manager returned. I thanked him for his time and left the store feeling even more confident that I would get the job.

After several days, I called back to ask if the manager was available. Time after time, I was told that he was in meetings or on the phone, and he would call me back. He never did. This went on for several days, and I began to think that he was giving me the runaround and had possibly hired someone else.

After a couple of weeks, I decided to take matters into my own hands, and I went back to the store to try to meet with the manager. As I walked around the store, I noticed just how busy the store really was. It was overflowing with customers, and the employees were all running around in a panic. After a few moments, I noticed that there was an accident on the paint aisle, in which someone had dropped several gallons of paint, which was now oozing down the aisle. The employees were screaming at each other trying to decide who should clean it up, and no one seemed willing to put forth the effort. I immediately sensed a golden opportunity and tracked down the manager.

When I met him, I immediately liked his personality. Despite all of the chaos that was going on around him, he still had a pleasant disposition. I approached him, extended my perfected confident handshake and introduced myself. "Hello, my name is Michael Taylor. I filled out an application a couple of weeks ago and thought I would stop in to see if you had made a decision."

He paused for a moment and said, "Are you the guy that was supposed to save me some money? My assistant told me about you. Sorry I haven't gotten back to you; it's been pretty hectic around here, and I simply have not had the time to review your application."

"Well, sir, it appears that you could really use my help right now.

I can see just how busy you are, so wouldn't this be a perfect opportunity for you to hire someone who can help you right now? Someone who could take some of the pressure off of you and your crew? I'm ready to jump right in and help out if you'd like."

"That's a pretty good attitude you have, son. What do you know about the lumber industry? Do you have any experience in sales?"

"To be completely honest, sir, I don't have any experience in this industry. But what I do have is a positive mental attitude, a love for learning, and a great work ethic. If you give me the job, I know that I can become a great asset to you and your company." (I learned that line from one of my business books.) "As a matter of fact, I'm willing to start at the bottom and work my way up if you will give me a chance. I'm even willing to go clean up that mess on your paint aisle that no one else seems to want to clean up."

HOW THE CONVERSATION BEGAN

"What mess on the paint aisle?"

"You might want to go see for yourself, sir. I noticed it on my way in." As he walked toward the paint aisle, I was praying that no one had begun cleaning it up. I had a feeling that if the mess was still there, it would increase my chances of getting the job. When we got there, the mess was worse than ever, and no one was doing anything about it. "What the hell happened over here? Why isn't anyone cleaning this up?"

"As I mentioned, sir, your crew is very busy. I'm willing to jump right in and clean up this mess if you'd like. All you have to do is say the word, and I'll get right to it."

"You really are persistent, aren't you? I may regret this, but I think I would like to give you the opportunity. I haven't reviewed your application yet, but I'm willing to take a chance on you. I want you to go to the back warehouse and get some cleaning supplies and begin cleaning up this mess. When you finish, I will review your application, and if everything checks out, you can have the job. Is that fair enough for you?"

"Absolutely sir. That is more than fair. I can assure you that you will not regret this decision."

After several hours, I had cleaned up the mess and gone a step further. I cleaned up and reorganized the entire aisle. When I had finished, the manager smiled approvingly and said that he was confident that I would do a great job. He said that he had a very good feeling about my abilities, and that I had proved him right with the way I cleaned up the mess.

At the end of the day, he had reviewed my application and wanted to know why I had not finished high school. Initially, I thought I would not get the job, but when I explained to him that I was possibly going back to school, he said something that totally caught me off guard. He told me that he thought it would be a good idea for me to get my diploma, but it was not necessary for me to move up within the company. He said that the company always hired from within, and the person that did the best job would receive the promotions and the highest salaries. Now that I had my foot in the door, it was completely up to me to determine how far I would go. He said that if I really applied myself, I could create a really good career with this company. I was so excited I couldn't contain myself. I was smiling like the Cheshire Cat, and I could not hold my excitement.

"Thank you so much for this opportunity. I feel extremely confident that this is the beginning of a long-term relationship, and I'm really looking forward to growing with the company. Thank you, thank you, thank you!"

"I want you to be here tomorrow at seven a.m. Don't be late. I'll have your weekly schedule ready for you then. We will also discuss your salary and other benefits. Have a great evening and I'll see you tomorrow."

As I was driving home, I knew that I had just received my big break. This was the opportunity I had been waiting for. All of my dreams were about to come true. I was one step closer to fulfilling my destiny.

When I got home and shared the good news with my mom, she had a sense of cautious optimism. She could tell how excited I was, and like any mother, she began to drill me with questions about the company.

HOW THE CONVERSATION BEGAN

"How much are they going to pay you she asked?"

" The ad said that they pay 800 dollars a month plus commission. We are going to talk about the specifics tomorrow. The good news is that it's a full-time job with lots of benefits and room for advancement. The manager said that there is even a possibility that I can move into management."

"You should be very careful. A lot of companies will tell you certain things at the beginning just to get you to work hard. Then some of them will not keep up their end of the bargain. Did he say that you will need a college degree to move into management?"

"That's the really good news. He said that if I work hard and proved myself, I do not even need a high school diploma. He said that the company always hires from within, and now that I have a position with them, I can make my own destiny. My success with them is completely up to me."

"I'm not sure if I believe that, but I'll just wait and see. Congratulations on your new job. I'm proud and happy for you. Just remember everything I've taught you. Work hard, be honest, be smart, and care for others. If you do these things, you will always be successful.

That night, I could barely sleep. I couldn't wait to go to work. I had my first real job, and I was ready to take on the world. I finally fell asleep dreaming of making my first million dollars.

The next day, I made sure that I got to work early. I wanted to make a good first impression on my new co-workers. I immediately had a good relationship with the assistant manager. He and I became good friends, and he taught me a lot.

During the first few months, I learned a lot about the company. I was excited about learning as much as I could. I became a sponge for information and devoured all of the information that I was presented with. I learned about plumbing, electrical, hardware, lumber, paint, and building materials. My favorite part of the job was customer service. I really enjoyed helping people with their problems and providing them with solutions. Great customer service was my specialty, and it wasn't long before I was being recognized for being so customer friendly. I received my first raise within three months, and it really let me know that my manager was right about the company. Whoever worked the hardest would be compensated the most. My hard work was definitely paying off. Within six months, my manager asked me if I were interested in their assistant-manager training program. He said that he was confident that I had the intelligence, drive, and determination to eventually become a store manager, and he wanted to do everything he could to help me achieve this goal. I told him that I was definitely interested and had set the goal of becoming a manager one day.

Everything in my life was going smoothly. I had a really good job, I had moved into my own apartment, and I was learning a lot about the building-material industry as well as management. I was still reading tons of books about management and success, and I knew that I was on track to eventually live my dreams. Although I enjoyed working for this company, deep down inside, I knew that eventually, I wanted to be my own boss. I intuitively knew that this job would serve as a stepping stone to my ultimate dream.

After approximately a year, I was offered an assistant-manager position in another city. Initially, I did not want to move, but I knew that if I really wanted to get to the next level, I had to go. I accepted the offer and decided to move. By this time, I was really looking towards the future. I was on a fast track to success, and the next thing I decided was that I needed to start a family. I decided that it was time to get married. Although I was only twenty-one, I felt responsible and mature enough to start a family. As a matter of fact, my girlfriend at the time had a son from a previous relationship, and so I was marrying into a ready-made family. I felt up to the challenge, so I got married and started the next chapter of my life.

Once I moved and became an assistant manager, the responsibilities increased, and so did the work load. But I absolutely loved the challenge. All of the reading and seminars I had attended were paying huge dividends, as I was climbing the corporate ladder. I felt confident in my ability to delegate, communicate and articulate as a manager. I felt like a fish *in* water and was very comfortable being in a leadership position.

Although my work life was doing well, there were challenges at home that I was in complete denial about. Although I didn't really feel that unhappy, there were several issues in my marriage that I really needed to address. The problems started with minor arguments about my working too much and focusing too much attention on making money. I rationalized it by saying that it was the only way for us to move up the social and economic ladder. I always argued that I was doing it for my family and that my wife should understand and support me. Instead of dealing with the real problems, I simply worked harder at work and rationalized that whatever problems there were, I could fix them by making more money and becoming a manager. I focused all of my energy on moving up the ladder, and within six months, I received another promotion to a store in a different city.

I now had a reputation for being one of the best assistant managers in the company. The word was out that management was keeping a close eye on me and that I was on track to become a manager pretty soon. I continued to work hard and give a hundred percent; I knew that I was getting close. Approximately a year later, I received the call that I was going to be a manager. Words cannot express the joy and feelings of accomplishment I felt when I received that call. All of the books I read, seminars I attended, and late-night working hours had paid off. I was now a *manager*!

As I reflected back on the previous three years of my life, I recognized that I had done what few people had done before me. I had dropped out of high school yet had succeeded in the business world and proved that anything was possible if I set my mind to it. I had overcome the odds, and I had won. I felt a deep sense of pride, but at the same time, I knew that I had not reached my ultimate destiny.

I was only twenty-two years old at the time that I made manager. I was the youngest manager the company had had in its fifty-seven-year history. It was a great accomplishment and one that I am still proud of today some twenty-four years later.

As a result of being promoted, I moved closer to my ultimate goal. I had gained a tremendous amount of knowledge in business, and now I would have an opportunity to apply the things I had learned. Being a manager turned out to be the highlight of my young life. I had gained the respect and admiration of my peers, and of course, my mom was proud beyond words to see her baby living the American Dream. I had succeeded in my quest to become a manager, but I knew that my life was just beginning. During this time, I knew that I needed to keep my promise to my mom of getting my diploma. Although I knew that I really did not "need" the diploma, there was a part of me that felt like something was missing. I knew that I needed to fill this void, so I enrolled in a program to receive my GED. Although my mother was extremely proud of my becoming a manager, without question, she was more proud of the fact that I kept my promise to her and received my high-school diploma. I must admit that I, too, felt a deep sense of pride and accomplishment. Of course, I knew that education is a life-long process. Although I had no intention of going to college, I committed myself to lifelong learning. I knew that this was the key to my success. Even today, I continue my commitment to constant and never-ending improvement.

At the age of twenty-three, I purchased my first home and had my first child with my wife. I felt like a responsible adult for the first time in my life. With the home and child came all of the responsibilities of being a grown-up. Mortgages, insurance, car notes, and the responsibility of managing a multi-million dollar company were all new to me, but I was up to the challenge. I was able to take all of the knowledge and wisdom I had gained in pursuit of being successful and apply them to my life. As a result, the first three years went rather smoothly.

When I was twenty-six, my wife and I had our second child together, and on the surface, it looked as if we were the perfect American couple. We had the house, the cars, the kids, the career, and everything society says we're supposed to have to be successful, but there was something definitely wrong with our perfect family picture. The American Dream was beginning to turn into the American Nightmare.

I will admit that we were actually pretty comfortable for a couple of years, but then the economy turned for the worse, and there were several financial challenges that I had to deal with for the very first time. In addition to the financial challenges, there were still the unresolved issues in my marriage that I had been avoiding for a very long time. Those issues had finally caught up with me, yet I was still unwilling to deal with them directly. As a result of my denial, my marriage began to unravel.

As I write this, I am speaking from the point of retrospective reflection. At the time, I was so focused on making money and having a career that I had completely distanced myself from my wife. Of course, at the time, I was completely unaware that I was doing this. I did not recognize that I was emotionally unavailable to her and that I was actually using my work as a way to cover up my own deep-seated emotional issues. What I know now is that I was not able to give her what she really needed: emotional and spiritual support and connection. She really didn't care about the titles, the money, the house or the vacations. What she really wanted and needed was me. Nothing more. She would have been just as happy living in an apartment driving a used car without any participation in social activities. She simply wanted to love me and be my wife, and that was enough for her. But I could not comprehend or accept that. As a result of my own insecurities, I attacked her and made her wrong for simply trying to love me. I rationalized by accusing her of not appreciating how hard I was working. I blamed everything on her and did not take responsibility for being a large part of the problem.

It truly amazes me how I could have been so blind. I should have recognized that I was neglecting her emotional needs. I should have known that staying at work long hours, even when it was unnecessary, was a sure sign that there was something wrong. I should have known that our marriage could not improve unless I decided to open up and share what was really driving my behavior. And most of all, I should have recognized that I had given her everything except that which she needed the most. Me. But I didn't know. I didn't know that I was supposed to be emotionally available. I didn't know that men were supposed to be emotionally and spiritually connected to their wives. As a matter of fact, I didn't have a clue what any of that psychobabble even meant at the time. I didn't know; I didn't know; I just did not know.

As a result of my not knowing and denial, I distanced myself from my wife and ultimately ended up going through a divorce. I was in new territory for the first time in my life. I had failed at something, and it was an extremely difficult thing to admit. Without question, the most difficult aspect of my divorce was the overwhelming feeling of failure. My entire sense of self was wrapped up in the titles of manager, husband, and father, and as a result of losing my family, I lost my sense of self. None of the business books I had read prepared me for this. The time had come for me to move my life in a new and different direction because my life was definitely not working.

This is the point where *A New Conversation with Men* actually begins. I share that story with you because I believe every man can relate to it. We have all experienced disappointments and setbacks in our lives, and some of us are more resilient than others. The purpose of this book is to assist any man who may be struggling with life's difficulties and is looking for a way to put their life back together. The reason that I believe this book is so important is that most men will not speak openly about the emotional and psychological challenges we deal with on a daily basis, and my hope is that this book can be a beacon of hope for any man who is ready to hear itsmessage. I believe it is a book whose time has come, and I hope the insights and information prove valuable to you and your life.

Now back to the story.

As mentioned, my life was in chaos, and I was really struggling to keep myself together. All of the business and motivational books never prepared me for these types of challenges. No amount of motivation could help me deal with the incredible amount of loss and suffering I was going through. My heart ached, my mind was cloudy, and my soul felt split in half. I had lost all sense of my identity. My life was in a downward spiral, and I needed to get it back on track. But how was I supposed to do that? I was in unfamiliar territory, and it was extremely uncomfortable.

During the darkest period of my life, I had an amazing epiphany. While sitting up late one night, I was trying to figure out how to get my life back together. I was replaying all the events that led up to my downfall, and I could not fully comprehend what had actually happened. I concluded that I was really a good guy, and I shouldn't be suffering the way that I was. I didn't have a pity party, but I was really struggling with trying to find something positive to be learned from my failure. I tried to come up with something to be grateful for; all I could think about was being a failure.

But then the epiphany. I started to think about how I succeeded from the beginning. I reflected back on all of the books and seminars I had participated in. I replayed all of the events in my mind, and

I remembered how I had been so committed to society's version of success. I remembered how I had overcome many obstacles, and deep down inside, I knew that if I could succeed once, I could do it again. As I thought about all of my accomplishments and successes, I realized that during this time, I had actually lost touch with my joy. I had spent all of my energy building my intellect, but I had completely neglected my heart and soul. My work and my family life had become intellectual tasks devoid of any feeling or emotion. There was no happiness or joy in any part of my life. I knew that this was the reason I was so miserable, and I needed to do something immediately. I then asked myself the single most important question I had ever asked up to that point in my life.

The question was this: "What if I take all of the energy and effort I have used trying to get rich, into simply being happy?" This was the question that changed everything for me. In that moment, something inside of me shifted. I knew this was what I needed to do, so I set out on a quest to become authentically happy with me, myself, and I. It was a decision that would set the stage for me to ultimately find my purpose and my passions in life. It was ultimately the question that would lead me back to my joy! Although it wasn't easy, I can honestly say that I found that joy, and I am currently living my dream.

My journey to happiness began with my willingness to begin reading and studying different types of books and participating in different types of seminars. Instead of the intellectual, get-rich-quick, money-making, management-type books and seminars, I begin reading and participating in psychology, spirituality, and personal-development books and workshops. The difference was that these books and seminars challenged me to look within myself to discover the root causes of my behaviors. They helped me recognize that I was completely responsible for my own happiness, and the way I would experience that happiness was for me to look within myself. I have come to know that the answer to every question we have can be found within us if we are willing to look deeply inside ourselves and find them. And although this is a difficult and sometimes painful journey, it is the only way for us to get to a place of authenticity and freedom.

During this process, I asked myself another question, which also led me to my ultimate purpose and destiny. That question was, "What does it really mean to be a man in today's ever-changing society?" This turned out to be the granddaddy of all questions. It is the question that I have been trying to answer for the past twenty years. It is the question that challenged me to spend the last twenty years or so researching psychology, philosophy, metaphysics, religion, and spirituality trying to find an answer. It is the question that propelled me to become a writer, speaker, and radio-show host. I believe it is the question that every man in America should be asking himself right now.

What does it mean to be a man in today's ever-changing society?

This is the question that I believe can and will change the fabric of the world. By being willing to create a new conversation with men, I believe that we can eradicate the vast majority of challenges America faces. By creating a new paradigm of masculinity, I believe we lay the foundation for a country that fulfills its declaration of being the land of the free home of the brave.

This book is my attempt to change not only America but the world at large. I believe the time has come for us to embrace all of humanity and to work together to heal the planet. Men across the globe should be willing to participate in this new conversation, which ultimately should lead to a kinder, gentler, and more compassionate world. My belief is that the old ways of being a man no longer serve us, and we must create new ways of relating and participating with one another. This will not happen as a result of political or judicial means. It will only occur when we, as men, learn to embrace this new conversation that I am currently writing about.

For this conversation to weave itself into the consciousness of the world, we must heed the advice of Michael Jackson. We must start with the man in the mirror and ask him if he is willing to change his ways. If he is, then the new conversation begins. Are you willing to engage in the conversation? Are you willing to challenge your deep-rooted beliefs about what it means to be a man? Are you willing to look deeply at the man in the mirror? If the answer is yes, then you are already engaged in the conversation. As a matter of fact, if you've read this far, that tells me that you are already a member of our revolution. The truth of the matter is that most men are not ready for this dialog. Most men are content with living the lie and are too afraid to engage in this conversation. But if you are still reading, that tells me that you are ready. You are ready for the new conversation, and that is a reason for celebration. Welcome to the revolution; we've been waiting for you.

My hope is that this book becomes a guide for all men who are willing to live extraordinary life. Despite all of the challenges facing our world, I remain optimistic that there are better days ahead. Each of us must simply do our part by discovering who we really are and reaching our full potential. Once we come to the recognition of who we are, we must then take our gifts and talents and share them with others. Sharing our gifts and talents while expressing our joy is a surefire way to transform our world.

My commitment to you is to be as open, honest, and transparent as I can be while sharing the lessons I have learned. I can assure you that this book comes from my heart and is written with the sincerest intention. As you read the contents, simply listen to your own inner voice and see if the message resonates with you. The time is now for a new conversation. I'm glad you have decided to participate.

Just remember this quote as you read through this book:

Personal transformation leads to world transformation. Transform yourself, and you automatically transform others. Welcome to *A New Conversation with Men*!

"The basic difference between an ordinary man and a warrior is that a warrior takes everything as a challenge, while an ordinary man takes everything as a blessing or a curse."

— Carlos Castaneda

Chapter Two

Our Greatest Challenge

I would like you to take a moment and use your imagination. I'd like you to imagine that you are a human being from another planet in another dimension. On your planet, there is no violence, no prisons, no hatred, and no racism. There is no overcrowding, no global warming, no healthcare crisis, and no struggling economy, and everyone lives in complete peace and harmony. It is utopia by every definition of the word.

Now, imagine that your name is Mike, and you are currently a student in college. As a result of your hard work and good grades, you have been selected to take on a very special assignment. Your professor calls you into his office to explain what your assignment will be.

Professor: "Hello, Mike. Let me begin by thanking you for the contributions you have made to this university. Your exemplary grades and dedication to improving the lives of others are the reason you have been chosen to tackle this assignment."

Mike: "Thank you, sir. I look forward to this opportunity."

Professor: "Do you have any idea what this new assignment is about?" Mike: "No sir. I have no idea."

OUR GREATEST CHALLENGE

Professor: "Our scientists have discovered another planet that is very similar to ours. We aren't exactly sure of the location of this planet, but we are able to pick up their media broadcasts and it appears that they are very much like us. We do not have any video, so we're not sure what they look like, but based on what we have heard so far, we are assuming that they actually look just like us. What we need you to do is to listen to these broadcasts and write a report about how the men of their planet live and behave. We have decided to focus our attention on a country called America. Apparently, this country has a patriarchal structure that places men above women in almost every segment of their society. We are assuming that they have not yet evolved the way we have here, and we hope that your report will give us a better understanding as to why they appear to be so primitive in their thinking and behaviors. Are you willing to study these men and report back with your findings?"

Mike: "Yes sir. I am definitely looking forward to this assignment, and I can assure you that I will do everything in my power to learn everything I can about these men and report all of my findings and scientific conclusions back to the university. When do I get started?"

Professor: "You can start immediately. We have set up a special location for you to begin. Hopefully, you can complete the report within a month's time. Do you think this will give you enough time to complete a thorough report?"

Mike: "I'm not sure. I really won't know until I begin the study."

Professor: "That's understandable. Then I would like you to provide an update on your findings every seven to ten days. This will help us measure your progress and give us an indication of how long the full project will take. Is this acceptable?"

Mike: "Yes sir. I will begin immediately."

Professor: "I would like to introduce you to Julie. She will be assisting you with this report. She will teach you how to use the technology to access their media broadcasts and will be there to assist in any other capacity you may need."

Julie: "Hello, Mike. I'm really looking forward to assisting you." Mike: "Nice to meet you."

Professor: "It's time for you two to get started. Take some time to get acquainted and then begin the project as quickly as possible. Do not forget to report back to me every seven to ten days to keep me abreast of what you are finding. Good luck!"

Julie: "C'mon, Mike, I'll take you to the facility. It's not far from here." Mike: "So how did you get chosen for this project?"

Julie: "I wrote a book about life on other planets several years ago. At the time, everyone said that I was crazy. As a matter of fact, it actually cost me my teaching job. But then, when the scientists started picking up the signal from the planet Earth, they contacted me immediately to get my opinion. They then asked if I would assist you in creating this report."

Mike: "So you've always believed there was intelligent life on other planets?"

Julie: "Absolutely. When I look at the vast expansiveness of our universe, it has always been difficult for me to believe that our planet was the only one with intelligent life. It simply did not make sense to me."

OUR GREATEST CHALLENGE

Mike: "Well, it looks like you will be vindicated and possibly reinstated to your old teaching job as a result of this discovery. That should make you pretty happy."

Julie: "I'm really not concerned about my former job. I'm just really excited to know that there are other planets with intelligent life. Do you know what this means? It means we are not alone in this magnificent universe, and that is cause for celebration."

Mike: "I agree. I'm ready to get started."

Julie: "Well, we're here, so you get your wish. Let's take in our bags, have some lunch, and then get started."

Mike: "Sounds good to me."

The two students unpacked their belongings, had lunch and then got started.

Julie: "This is the machine that picks up the broadcast. All you do is put on the headphones and listen to their media sources. Apparently, they have twenty-four-hour-a-day news programs that give you up-to-date information on what's currently happening on their planet."

Mike: "Great. The first thing I want to do is to listen to some of their broadcasts so that I can get a sense of how the men on planet Earth behave. Is there a way to record these broadcasts?"

Julie: "Yes. It's already set up."

Mike: "We can record the broadcast, and I will take notes for the report. All right; I think I'm ready to begin. Let's tune into one of the broadcasts. Okay. I'm picking up a signal. I can hear the report coming across the airwaves. O, my gosh, it is a story about a man who walked onto a college campus and started shooting people at random.

He killed thirty-three people and then turned the gun on himself. That is so sad. Why do you think he would do such a thing?"

Julie: "I have no idea. We have not had a murder on our planet in over 300 years. I can't imagine that people on other planets are still killing each other. Let's try another broadcast and see what else we find."

Mike: "All right, I'll try a different station. Oh no! I can't believe this. There is a story about a man who was mad at his girlfriend so he killed her then chopped her up and grilled her remains on a bar-b-que pit. This can't be real. The men on planet Earth are extremely violent. I'm listening to another story, and there was a man who was upset at his girlfriend for breaking up with him, and guess what he did?"

Julie: "I'm afraid to ask."

Mike: "He went to her job, doused her with gasoline, and set her on fire. These men are so barbaric! Evidently, their species has not evolved, and they are still acting out in ways that our species hasn't acted in hundreds of years. This is very disturbing. I'm afraid to listen to another broadcast."

Julie: "Why don't you take a break and let me listen? Hopefully, I can find something different."

After a few moments, Julie screamed in terror. "Oh no, no, no! It can't be true. No man could ever do such a heinous thing. It's just not possible. This can't be happening."

Mike: "What happened?"

Julie: (sobbing) "There is a story of a man who raped a three-year-old girl. After he raped her, he strangled her and dumped her body in a field. The most disturbing part is that the little girl was his own daughter. How could a man do that to his own daughter? I do not believe I have ever heard of such a sinful act ever in my life. Who are these men of Earth?"

Mike: "I don't know, but I think it would be a good idea if we took a break. I have enough information to begin my report, and I really cannot take any more of this violence. I need to disconnect from all of this negativity so that I can be at peace. Let's call it a day, and we will start again tomorrow. Hopefully, the broadcast will not be so violent. "

Julie: "I totally agree. I can't remember a time when I have felt so saddened and upset after listening to a broadcast of any type. I am so glad that we do not have that type of violence here on our planet."

Mike: "I agree. Although I dislike what we have heard so far, I think it's important for us to continue this report. Maybe there is a way that we can help them remove the violence from their society if we find a way to eventually communicate with them. Maybe our report will actually help them. Let's get some rest and come back tomorrow."

The next day.

Mike: "Hello, Julie, how did you sleep?"

Julie: "It took me awhile to fall asleep because I couldn't get the media stories from the planet Earth out of my mind. After a few hours, I did fall asleep, but I didn't sleep very well."

Mike: "Me either. I can't remember a time when I had such difficulty getting to sleep. I'm definitely sure it was the result of absorbing all of that negative energy from the planet Earth's broadcasts. Hopefully, today will be better."

Julie: "I sure hope so."

Mike: "Let's get the equipment set up, and we can get started."

Julie: "Everything is ready. All you have to do is tune in the broadcast, and you can begin."

Mike: "Okay, here we go. I've decided to try another method. Yesterday, we tuned into television programs, so I thought today we would listen to some radio broadcast. I'm picking up a channel now. Apparently, it's some sort of talk show. They are talking about something called 'domestic violence.' Have you ever heard of such a thing?"

Julie: "No I haven't. What is that?"

Mike: "It sounds like domestic violence is what happens when someone you are supposed to love and care about inflicts bodily harm onto you, the person they are supposed to love. They are now saying that it does not have to be physical violence—it can also be emotional and psychological violence. The host says that men commit the overwhelming majority of domestic violence acts, but women can also be perpetrators of domestic violence."

Julie: "How can you inflict bodily harm onto someone you love? I really can't understand that. That type of behavior is so different from the behavior here on our planet. The people of Earth seem to actually enjoy violence."

Mike: "Although that is difficult to comprehend, I believe you are right. It appears that violence is so deeply rooted in their culture; they unconsciously accept it as the only way to live. I think I'll listen to some of their music. Maybe their music is different. Maybe there is music that they use to help them feel calm and at peace. Let me see if I can locate a music station. Aha, here is one. Let's listen to their music for a moment. I'm going to put the music on the speaker so that we can listen to it simultaneously. Listen to this."

Julie: "That's terrible! Why would they want to listen to that type of music? How can they listen to such vulgarity and profanity? No wonder their society is so violent. Just listen to those lyrics."

Mike: "I agree. I believe that their music has affected their behavior. How could it not? If they are all listening to that type of music, I can see why their society is so filled with anger and hatred. Those lyrics alone are enough to trigger violent acts in anyone who would listen to them on a regular basis. I'm going to take a break and write down some conclusions I've come to for the report. You can continue to listen if you like."

Julie: "No thank you. I'll turn it off for now. I would like to go outside and reconnect with nature. I need to put myself in a peaceful place if I'm going to continue listening to the people of Earth. All of their negativity really is affecting me."

For the next several days, the students have the exact same experience. Wherever they tune in, they are bombarded with messages of violence and negativity. After a week, it's time for them to file their first report on what they have found out about the men of Earth.

Professor: "Hello, Mike. Hello, Julie. I hear you have completed the first week of your assignment. What do you have to report?"

Mike: "Well, sir, the picture isn't pretty. The men of Earth appear to be violent beyond comprehension. Their society is so rooted in violence; I don't see how they could ever change. As far as I can tell, it's been like this since the beginning of their existence. They have a divine holy book which they call the Bible. It supposedly tells the story of how life began on their planet. It is supposed to be the inspired revelation from their Creator. They have taken this book and come up with different interpretations of it, and they call these interpretations religions. They then fight and kill each other over their interpretations of the same holy book. Even their most holy book is filled with incredible acts of violence. Several other books proclaim to be the inspired word of their Creator, but each book seems to proclaim that it is *The Book* from the divine. This has caused an incredible amount of violence and suffering on their planet. They each believe that their way is the right way, and they refuse to look at it from a higher, all-inclusive perspective the way we do on our planet."

Julie: "It's actually very sad. Some of the things they do to each other will break your heart. They not only hurt people they do not know, they also hurt the people they are supposed to love and cherish. It baffles my mind, and I would have never imagined life on another planet to be this way. After listening to these broadcasts for the last week, I have concluded that we are definitely a more evolved species, and the people of Earth have a long way to go if they are striving to create a utopian society like ours." Professor: Well, the next question we must begin asking ourselves is whether or not we should attempt to make contact with these people. If so, do you think we could teach them how to be more civil towards one another?" Mike: "I'm not really sure if that's possible. I have come to the conclusion that violence is probably rooted in their DNA somehow. I'm not sure how, but based on what I have listened to so far, there is no other explanation that I can come up with. I am so convinced of this; I will be able to complete my report in the next couple of days. I do not believe that there is any reason to continue this study, because the conclusion will be the same.

The men of Earth are inherently violent, and that will be the conclusion of my report.

"To answer your question about whether we can teach them to be more civil towards one another, my initial response would be no. I do not believe that the men of Earth are ready for change. I believe that they are so caught up in their old ways; it would be virtually impossible to get them to see things from a different point of view. I would be afraid to contact them and definitely afraid to possibly go to such a violent place."

Julie: "Although I believe that the men of Earth are violent, I also believe that they can change. I do not believe that they are inherently violent, and I do not believe that violence is coded in their DNA. My gut feeling is that if we can help them change their thinking about violence, then we can help them transcend that violence. Although the overwhelming majority of the broadcasts we heard were negative, there were definitely some reasons for hope and optimism."

Professor: "So what do you think our next step should be?"

Mike: "Although I disagree with Julie's assessment, I have had a change of heart. I would like to work with her to try to contact the men from Earth. If our society can evolve, I must believe that other societies can do the same. I think it would be a good idea to try to contact the men from Earth and see if we can assist with their evolution."

Julie: "Wow, Mike, that's great! I would definitely like to try to contact the men from Earth to help them evolve. I think we make a great team, and eventually, if we are able to contact them, I believe we could have a positive impact on their world."

Professor: "Let me take a moment to thank each of you for your willingness to take on this assignment. I know how difficult it must have been to subject yourself to listening to such random acts of violence. It will be important for both of you to take some time off to remove any negative residual thoughts and feelings you may have as a result of this assignment. You are hereby free to take a few weeks off to relax and reward yourself. You have both been awarded an all-expenses-paid vacation of your choice anywhere in our world. Just name the place, and we'll make sure you get there.

"In the meantime, we will be working with our scientists to see if we can devise a way to contact the men from Earth. Once we do, we will contact you and decide on our next course of action. Thanks again for your efforts."

I believe that this story is a metaphor for our perception of men in our society. Because of the overwhelming exposure of violence throughout our media, I believe most people will say that men are intrinsically and inherently violent. If you will turn on any media broadcast, you will see what I mean. Although this was a fictional story, each broadcast that Mike and Julie listened to were actual events that have occurred right here in America. So based on all of these negative stories, it's easy to see how most people have concluded that all men are violent. And if you happen to be from another planet or culture, for that matter, it would be easy to justify your conclusion about men and violence in this country.

OUR GREATEST CHALLENGE

With all of the negative images of men in our society, we are faced with a major dilemma. How do we not only change the perception but change the behaviors of men in our society? How do we get men to stop killing each other? How do we get men to be better fathers, husbands, lovers, and friends? How do we remove greed and corruption from a man's mind and help him recognize that he is complete and whole without any external possessions or positions? How do we get men to become more nurturing, caring, compassionate, and loving?

The overwhelming majority of people will say that it's just not possible. They will point to all of the evidence that statesmen cannot and will not change. They will call in experts and throw out countless statistics that support their ideas and beliefs, and most of all, they will say that I am absolutely insane to assume that anything can be done to resolve the aforementioned challenges.

Although getting men to change their behaviors may appear to be an insurmountable task, I actually believe that it's possible. And the solution to all of the challenges facing men is actually rather simple. Now, I must make the distinction between something being simple and something being easy. They are definitely not the same. And though my proposed solutions may be simple, they may also be the most difficult thing any man will ever do. Would you like to know what my solution is?

My simple solution is this, we must have *A New Conversation with Men*! I'm sure you're wondering what this means, so let me explain. Although we are constantly bombarded with negative images of men in our society, I personally believe that men are not inherently violent, and they can change. I believe that our media will always focus on the dysfunction and negativity of our society, but I also believe that the media gives you a very small glimpse of what's really happening in our world. For every negative, violent story in our media, there are literally thousands, even millions of positive ones. Unfortunately, we live in such a violent culture that the media's focus will always be violent. The media's motto is, "If it bleeds, it leads," meaning that violent news is given primary importance by our media; that is how they present their programming. But the fact of the matter is that they will only show what people will watch, so we can't blame the media, because they are actually giving society what it asks for. Whether we will admit it or not, this country loves violence. It is absolutely addicted to it. If you do not believe me, simply take a look at our society as a whole.

Our movies, our music, our judicial system, and even our families are filled with violence. If we didn't love violence so much, our society would reflect that. Results do not lie, and our results say we love and support violence. This is where a *New Conversation with Men* comes in. In order for us to remove the violence in our society, we must first begin with dialog. Dialog is always the first step to change; it is the door to societal transformation. Unfortunately, the overwhelming majority of people (especially men) are not willing to walk through this door and engage in this dialog, so it's up to the few brave souls who are courageous enough to begin this new conversation to lead by example. If you are reading this book, then I believe that you are one of those brave souls.

At this point, I would like to interject that I happen to be an irrepressible optimist. In case you haven't noticed, I have great faith in humanity, and my perception of the world is a lot different from what you may see in the media. Amazingly, people like me are called unrealistic dreamers. People say that optimists are in denial and disillusioned and should be locked up and kept away from the mainstream. But I beg to differ. I say that never has the need been greater for optimistic people to speak out and provide a different perspective on the current events that are happening in our world. Our world needs dreamers who are willing to go against the status quo and begin the great shift in consciousness that will ultimately change our world for the better. If you agree with me, then I'd like to welcome you to a new conversation with men.

Now, let's take a look at what we are up against. Let's examine some of the challenges currently facing our world and then see how we can apply a new conversation to create some solutions.

As the current presidential race grabs the headlines, there are three primary challenges that the candidates propose they can fix. What's currently at the top of the list is the economy, next comes health care, and then comes the war in Iraq. Following these challenges are our educational system, poverty, and then global warming. Of course, these are just my observations, and they may or may not be what the politicians are saying. But for the sake of argument, let's say that these are the greatest challenges facing America right now:

The economy Health care The Iraq War

Public education Poverty

Global warming

Based on our current political structure, these are issues that politicians promise they can fix. If you ask 100 people, "What is the greatest challenge facing America today?" I'm pretty certain that one of these things would come up possibly 90% of the time.

But if you asked me, my answer would be completely different. If I were asked what I believe to be the greatest challenge in America (and the world abroad), my response would be, "I believe that the greatest challenge facing America today is to redefine masculinity." Redefining masculinity means that we recognize the fact that the old ways of being a man no longer work. By embracing new ways of being men, we lay the foundation for the eradication of all six of the challenges mentioned above. We must be willing to create a new paradigm of masculinity in which men let go of antiquated ideas of manhood and embrace new, more evolved ways of behaving and relating to each other.

Before you dismiss my idea, let me explain how redefining masculinity can actually assist in resolving those six challenges I mentioned.

Let's start with the economy. It amazes me when I hear politicians promise that they are going to create jobs. I'm not going to attack the politicians, but I do have one question for them, "If you create these jobs, what happens if the people do not have the skills and training to fill these positions you create? How will that benefit the economy?

My point is this. Politicians are not responsible for your success. You are. I do not care who the president is, if you aren't willing to gain the necessary skills to advance your career and improve the quality of your life, you will ultimately fail. On the other hand, if you embrace a new conversation with men, and you gain the motivation and inspiration to reach your fullest potential, then you can create the career of your dreams. This will ultimately make you more money, which you will ultimately spend, which will then boost the economy. Simple but not easy!

Now, let's talk about health care. Let's imagine that our government passes new healthcare legislation, and everyone in America has healthcare. Does this mean that everyone will use it? The fact of the matter is that most men that currently have health insurance today don't even use it. So even if there were access to healthcare, most men are reluctant to take advantage of it. Once again, I assert that in a new conversation with men, men learn to take better care of their physical bodies. They learn to move through the fear and embarrassment of seeing a doctor, and they make a commitment to being healthy. By redefining masculinity, men learn to be open and honest about what ails them, and they then take action to take care of their health. Simple but not easy!

So, what about the war in Iraq? It's actually pretty simple. Men have always been conditioned to be warriors and aggressors. By embracing this new conversation with men, men will learn to set aside their inflated egos and their need to be right and be more open and receptive to non-violent solutions to our challenges. In this new paradigm of masculinity, men will learn to be more caring, compassionate, and loving. Make love, not war! Simple but not easy!

Then there is the issue of public education. Did you know that approximately 70% of all high-school dropouts come from fatherless homes? If we are going to turn around our educational system, we must address this issue. In a new conversation with men, men learn to be better fathers. In doing so, I believe we can improve our educational system by having our youth better prepared for school because they have been raised in loving, supportive family settings. In addition, we will have men more actively involved in our educational system, which will provide positive role models for our youth. Simple but not easy!

What about poverty? One of the contributing factors to poverty is single-parent homes. When we can empower men to be better husbands and fathers, we begin to establish close-knit family units. When we have close-knit family units, we can break the cycles of poverty and begin new generations of emotionally, psychologically, and financially well-adjusted children. By engaging in a new conversation with men, men will also learn to gain the skills necessary to secure jobs that pay well and careers that are fulfilling. This is how you eradicate poverty. Simple but not easy!

And last but not least, there is global warming. In a new conversation with men, men learn to respect and appreciate the beauty and the majesty of nature. By developing a deep reverence for the Earth, men will be less likely to do anything that harms the environment. With this new commitment of cleaning up the Earth, men will work together to come up with concrete solutions to the challenges facing our planet. Simple but not easy! Can you now see just how important this new conversation really is?

Can you grasp the implications of what this type of shift would do for our country? Our world? Can you see my vision of a new conversation with men? In this vision, men would be empowered to discover and express their own unique gifts and talents. Once they recognize who they really are they would then be able to create this new paradigm that I'm writing about. High divorce rates, drug and alcohol addiction, corporate corruption, senseless acts of violence, and child abuse would all be issues of the past, and this new conversation would begin creating a brighter future. Just remember, simple but definitely not easy. Improbable but definitely possible.

As you read through these simple but not easy solutions, be sure to understand that in no way am I minimizing or trivializing the challenges facing our country. Without question, there are enormous challenges ahead, but I honestly believe that we can overcome these challenges. As I mentioned, these challenges aren't really political. They are actually emotional, psychological, and spiritual in nature. And until we address them as such, we will never solve them. *A New Conversation with Men* is my attempt to provide insights and information that challenges men (and women) to embrace a new way of thinking and behaving on this planet. These aren't just American challenges; they are human challenges. We must all work together regardless of race, religion, or ethnicity. The human race is our family, and we must embrace each and every member regardless of where they may live on planet Earth.

So, now that I have talked a little about the societal challenges, I will now shift the conversation to a more personal level. In all sincerity, this is the level at which we can change the world. Personal transformation leads to world transformation, and it is entirely up to you to take on this challenge. Once you transform yourself, it is incumbent upon you to assist others in doing the same thing. This is the reason that I wrote *ANCWM*. I believe it is my responsibility to uplift humanity and be a light in a seemingly dark world by sharing the insights and information that have made me a better man.

The first thing you must do is decide to wake up and become conscious. Although that may sound easy, it is without question, the most difficult thing you will probably ever do. Becoming conscious means that you become willing to look deep within your own heart, mind and soul to discover the limiting beliefs that you may have about yourself and the world around you. You must be willing to gain a new understanding of how our society works and how it affects so many of your behaviors.

Let's begin by taking a quick look at how and why so many men struggle with life and with living. Have you ever asked yourself, "What does it mean to be a man?" Have you ever wondered why men are the way they are? These are some of the questions I have been asking myself for the past twenty years, and as I mentioned in the previous chapter, I do not pretend to have all the answers. However, I would like to share some lessons and wisdom I have gained in answer to that question.

First of all, I believe three things shape a man's view of the world and of himself. These three things shape his belief systems about what it means to be a man and ultimately define his reality. By gaining a deeper understanding of these three things, I believe we begin creating a foundation for change. These three things are:

Our Families Our Culture
Our Media/Society

Family

The first thing that affects our beliefs about being a man is our families. If you were raised in a family in which you were exposed to a caring, nurturing, and supportive father and mother, then there is a good chance that your beliefs about being a man will reflect that reality. On the other hand, if you were brought up in a family in which men were uncaring, violent, and distant, then the chances are you will exhibit some of those same behaviors. The good news here is that no matter what environment you may have been brought up in, you can still change your behaviors if you choose to. The overwhelming majority of behaviors are learned, and therefore, they can be unlearned, and that is one of the premises of this book. To possibly help you unlearn any unwanted negative behaviors that may be keeping you from reaching your full potential, it's important that you begin to recognize the environment you were raised in because ultimately, it will assist you in changing your behavior if necessary. But remember, your past does not have to dictate your future, and therefore, you can heal and learn from your past and not let it affect your present or your future.

Culture

Your culture includes things like your racial identity, your religious upbringing, the clothes you wear, the music you listen to, the food you eat, and the way you interact with the world. All of these things shape and mold you into the man that you are now. Your family is really just an extension of your culture. In some cultures, men are comfortable with embracing one another and even kissing one another on the cheek. Yet in other cultures, those same actions are viewed as being overly sensitive and weak. Therefore, it should be easy to understand how men from different cultures act out in different ways.

Media and Society

Last but definitely not least, we have possibly the most powerful influence on our beliefs and our behaviors. That is our media and society. Instead of using the words "media" and "society," I would like to use the metaphor of "the drift" as I speak about this influence. You see, I believe most people are stuck in "the drift," and they are completely unaware of it. I believe the majority of people are floating aimlessly along this current of conformity, and they have no idea where they are going. They simply choose to "go with the flow," which means they follow all of society's rules that supposedly will lead them to happiness and success.

This is the trap that most men get caught in, and now I would like to explain why we do this. When I was climbing the corporate ladder of success, my driving motivation was to make money. Although I considered myself to be a good husband and father, if I am completely honest with myself, I must admit that making money was my primary objective. Although I wasn't over-materialistic, I did believe that by having money, position, and power, then ultimately I would be happy. So I worked extremely hard to have the house, the wife, the kids, the vacations, the cars and all the other "stuff" that "the drift" says we are supposed to have in order to be successful. On the outside, it looked as if I was living the American dream, but on the inside, there was a completely different story.

OUR GREATEST CHALLENGE

So why did I end up losing it all? Because I was caught up in the drift and trying to live my life according to its rules. Instead of listening to my own heart, and understanding myself, I unconsciously bought into the drift's interpretation of success. You see, the drift will convince you that if you want to be happy, then you must accumulate "stuff." It says that if you love someone, you express that love by giving them "stuff." According to the drift, whoever has the most stuff wins the game, and as men, we definitely want to win the game. This belief has caused an incredible amount of pain and suffering in men's lives, and the time has come for us to have a new conversation with one another so that we can break free from the drift.

In order to break free from the drift, you must understand that it is your conscious and unconscious beliefs that keep you trapped within it. Your beliefs are simply the lenses through which you see the world. There is a beautiful saying, "If you change the way you look at things, the things you look at will change." This simply means that if you will change what you believe about the world, you will then change how you experience it. Your beliefs are what create your reality and your experience, so if you want to change any aspect of your life, you must be willing to change your beliefs first. This is a man's greatest challenge, being willing to examine his beliefs and then make a conscious and concerted effort to change them if needed. Remember what I said about "simple but not easy"? This statement definitely applies to that principle. But I can assure you that it is the only way to make permanent changes in your life.

A New Conversation with Men is designed to help you "rewrite the mental scripts" about what it means to be a man. This is what I mean by creating a new paradigm of masculinity, changing the conscious and unconscious beliefs that we hold on to as a result of our families, our culture and our society. By changing our beliefs, I believe we can change our world. Throughout this book, you will have the opportunity to examine and challenge your beliefs and scripts about being a man. My hope is that you will be willing to change the beliefs that no longer serve you and accept some new beliefs that will definitely empower you. As mentioned, this is not an easy undertaking. But for those of you who are willing to take it on, I can assure you that your life can be filled with love, joy, contentment, and unlimited possibilities. The question you must now ask yourself is, "Am I ready for a new conversation with men?" If you answered yes, then you have already taken on your greatest challenge.

Welcome to the revolution. We've been waiting for you.

> "The people who are crazy enough to think they can change the world, are the ones who do."
>
> — Steve Jobs

Chapter Three

The Five Illusions of Manhood

This quote by Steve Jobs is one of my absolute favorites. The reason that I love this quote so much is that all of my life, people have called me crazy, not in a bad way, but simply in a different way. In my heart and soul, I have always felt "different," not better than or less than anyone else, simply different from everyone else. As I reflect back on my life I recognize that I have always been that round peg trying to fit into the square hole of society. I truly believe that I can change the world. Maybe not in the way that Martin Luther King Jr. or Ghandi or Nelson Mandela changed the world, but in my own simple way, on my own simple terms, I can and I will change the world.

Although this may sound a bit grandiose, I believe that everyone actually has the ability and capacity to change the world. We all have the ability, but very few of us have the willingness. What sets us "crazy" people apart is simply our willingness to act on our abilities.

So what about you? Are you one of the crazy people? Are you crazy enough to believe that you can change the world? Are you willing to use your abilities to assist me in creating this new paradigm of masculinity that I'm writing about? Are you ready to fully engage in a new conversation with men and become a part of our new revolution? I believe you are, so let's examine the five illusions of manhood that every man must now be made aware of. Once men wake up from these illusions, I can assure you that a shift in male consciousness will occur, and the world will be transformed for the better.

As a result of the research and studying I've done over the past twenty years, I have concluded that there are five illusions that men hold onto that cause the overwhelming majority of pain and suffering in their lives. These illusions are perpetuated through our families, our cultures and our media. In other words, these illusions are actually an integral aspect of being caught in the drift. In order to break free from these illusions, a man must first become aware that they even exist. So I would like to share these five illusions with you now:

To be a man, you must be non-emotional and disconnected. To be a man, you must have status, positions, and power.

To be a man, you must have money and material possessions.

To be a man, you must use sexual conquest as a gauge for manhood. To be a man, you must win at all costs and compete against other men.

These five illusions are the foundation of all pain and misery in a man's life. If you will take a moment and really examine them, I believe you will see what I mean. To give you a better understanding of how these illusions affect your life, I will now break them down and explain each one individually.

To be a man, you must be non-emotional and disconnected.

I believe that this is the greatest illusion. All other illusions are actually built on top of this one. In our society, males are conditioned from a very young age to not feel. We are given the messages that to feel and express those feelings is somehow weak, or worse, feminine. Therefore, we start accepting this illusion even as little boys. Think about the powerful messages you received as a young boy; things like, "Big boys don't cry," "Stop being a baby," and "Don't act like a sissy" are the beginning of the acceptance of this illusion. What actually occurs is that we begin to shut down our emotions, and the only way to cope is to express ourselves through our intellect. We stop expressing how we feel, and we begin expressing what we think. Of course, there is absolutely nothing wrong with thinking. Using our intellect is an integral and necessary aspect of our humanity, but without our emotions, we become empty, hollow, automatons and miss out on the most important aspect of our lives.

This illusion is powerful because as men, we accept that the only appropriate feelings we should express are the negative ones. It's absolutely acceptable for a man to express anger and rage in our society without being accused of being less than a man, but if a man expresses joy, sadness, or fear, then his masculinity will always be questioned. A good example of this is a television interview with Terrell Owens, who is a wide receiver for the Dallas Cowboys football team. After the Cowboys suffered an emotional loss to the New York Giants, Terrell was defending his friend and quarterback Tony Romo. In the interview, Terrell began to cry as he shares openly about how unfair the media was being to his friend. It was obvious that he was deeply saddened by the loss, but he was also saying just how much he cared for his friend. As a result of this interview, his masculinity was immediately challenged. The media went into a frenzy about Terrell's emotional interview. Some of the sportscasters accused him of being weak and overly sensitive while others even questioned his sexuality by implying that he might be gay.

The question I pose to you is, why is it so unacceptable in our society for a man to be emotional? Does it really make us less than men if we are comfortable expressing our feelings and wear our hearts on our sleeves? Who decided that women could be emotional but not men?

This is accepted in our society because we are trapped in the illusion that men are supposed to be non-emotional and disconnected. It is an illusion that has been passed down for generations, and the time has come for us to wake up from this illusion. When a man is trapped in this illusion, he loses his ability to truly experience life the way it was meant to be. Without his emotions, he will miss out on the most important aspects of his life. His joy, passion, creativity, intuition, connection with his spouse, children, and even his faith are all connected to his ability to feel, so it is important that we break free from this illusion and create a new paradigm in which men are comfortable expressing their emotions openly and honestly without fear of having our masculinity challenged.

To be a man, you must have status, positions and power.

Have you ever noticed how our society adores celebrities, sports figures, and executives? We are taught that "He who has the gold makes the rules," which implies that the more money you have, the "better" you are as a person. The implication is that somehow, men who are wealthier or who have higher social status are somehow "superior" to other men. This is definitely an illusion. The truth of the matter is that monetary wealth does not make you a better man. It may, in some ways, make your life easier, but it definitely does not make a man superior to other men. The sad part of it is that too many men accept this illusion, and they spend all of their energy trying to move up the societal ladder to validate themselves. They invest all of their time and energy in trying to gain titles and labels, while in reality, they feel empty and unfulfilled. The way they try to compensate for this emptiness is by acting "superior" even though they really aren't. I must admit that I was definitely caught in this illusion twenty years ago. Although I did not consider myself to be superior to any other man, I did believe that attaining the title of "Manager" would somehow validate me as a man. Although I did not recognize it at the time, my ambition and drive was actually fueled by my own insecurities about being a man. In my mind, climbing the corporate ladder and becoming successful was a way to prove to myself that I was competent and intelligent. Unfortunately, even after I made it to the top, I still felt the same insecurities. Even though I put up the façade of being in control and in charge, there was a part of me that was a frightened little boy simply trying to find his way home.

Too many men are currently caught in this illusion of manhood. You can recognize them by their big egos and their arrogance. They parade around town flashing their titles at you and trying to get the external validation they so desperately need. On the outside, they may appear to have it all together, but on the inside, they are wounded little boys doing the best they can to maintain their charade.

To be a man, you must have money and material possessions.

This illusion is the reason men spend billions upon billions of dollars buying "stuff." Too many of us believe that if we just buy the right house, the right car, the right watch, or the right clothes, then we will be viewed as men, and we will gain approval from our friends. This is the reason so many of us feel empty and discontented because we have bought into the illusion that if we accumulate enough "stuff", we will feel fulfilled. Nothing could be further from the truth. This illusion is why so many of us try to "Keep up with the Joneses."

As I think about this illusion, I'm reminded of my high school days when I purchased my first car. My first car was a 1969 Ford Mustang that I absolutely loved. But it wasn't the freedom that came from owning my own car that excited me: it was the fact that in my mind, I had now become a man. Of course, I was only seventeen at the time and still living at home, but in my mind, I had graduated from adolescence and moved into manhood. (This just goes to show you how this particular illusion really kicks in around our formative high school years.)

Another way that I bought into this illusion was by pretending that I had lots of money even when I didn't. I remember keeping a big wad of cash in my pocket at all times, and I would always have a twenty or a fifty-dollar bill on top with lots of one-dollar bills on the bottom. Whenever I would be out with my friends, I would pull out my wad of cash and pretend that I had a lot more money than I actually did. Since most of my friends didn't have jobs or money, I was always seen as

"The Man" by my peers. This was definitely a big boost for my ego but it caused me to fall deeper and deeper into the illusion.

These are just two examples of the things some of us as men do when we are trapped in this illusion. Sadly, there are currently lots of men out there today who are still doing the things I did in high school. (Are you one of them?). They are the ones who have become trapped in the illusion that they must have money and material things to be a man, and I can assure you that they are paying a significant price in terms of their emotional, psychological and spiritual well-being.

To be a man, you must use sexual conquest as a gauge for manhood.

If you get nothing else from this book, my hope is that you will get this. This is one of the most destructive illusions perpetuated throughout our society. This illusion contributes to teenage pregnancy, divorce, rape, sexually transmitted diseases, and all sorts of violence. I cannot pinpoint when this illusion began, but I would assume that it has been around since the beginning of time. It really doesn't matter when it started; the question we must ask ourselves is how can we end it?

Think back to your youth and see if you remember how prevalent this illusion was, especially during your younger days. Do you remember when you were young and the only thing you thought about was sex? As a teenager, our minds and our hormones were obsessed with the prospect of having sex. If we are really honest with ourselves, we will recognize that almost everything we did in some way led to us trying to attract the opposite sex so that we could engage in the act of sex. We bought our cars to try to attract girls. We played sports hoping that it would attract girls. We bought clothes and kept our hair perfect in hopes of attracting girls. We made money to impress and attract girls. So why were we so obsessed with girls? Because we wanted to have sex! We all believed that by having sex, we would validate our manhood, and our friends would cheer for us, and we would be happy and fulfilled. So if we weren't having sex, we usually lied about it just to make sure that we maintained the illusion that we were real men. If we weren't having sex and maintaining this illusion, then we usually felt inadequate and somehow inferior as young men.

Now, I would like you to fast forward to the present. If you will take a moment and ask yourself the same questions, you will see that most of us as men are still trapped in the same illusion. We buy cars to attract women. We play sports to attract women. We buy clothes and keep our hair perfect to attract women. We make money and spend money to attract and impress women. So why are we so obsessed with attracting women? Because we want to have sex with women!

And when we aren't having sex with women, we're usually lying about it to our friends. Can you see the insanity in this? Sexual conquest does not make you a man. It is only an illusion and a temporary fix to your unhappiness. If you are using sex as a gauge for manhood, you are trapped in a vicious cycle of addiction and denial.

To be a man, you must win at all costs and compete against other men.

This is probably the least recognized of all the illusions. Although we seldom talk openly about this, there is an unspoken male law that says that we are supposed to always compete against one another. This can be witnessed on a large scale by corporate corruption. When a man's ego gets inflated, he will do any and everything to "stay on top." All rational thinking will go out the window if a man thinks that his competitor is getting ahead of him. Our business schools would teach you that being competitive is the foundation of success, but they will not teach you about the consequences of this overly competitive, macho position that too many men fall victim to.

A perfect example of this on a small scale is an experience I had as a salesman in a hardware store. One day, I sold a customer a very expensive bar-b-que grill. The customer wanted to make sure that it had all of the latest technology, and he wanted it to be the "best." I worked with him for a couple of days until I finally put together the grill of his dreams. As he walked out of the store, his final comment to me was, "Thanks for helping me put together such an awesome grill. My neighbor is going to be green with envy."

A couple of days later, a gentleman shows up and asks to speak to me about purchasing a grill. He specifically asked for me because his neighbor told him that I was very helpful. He raved about how awesome his neighbor's grill was and he said he wanted to purchase one just like it. But then he added that he wanted to make sure that it had at least one feature that his neighbor's grill did not have. He did not care what the feature was; as a matter of fact, he even mentioned that he probably wouldn't use the new feature, he simply wanted to make sure that it was better than his neighbor's grill.

This is what happens when you get caught in this illusion. You will do irrational things and then rationalize them by saying you work hard for your money, and you deserve to have the best. Of course, there is nothing wrong with wanting the best for yourself, but when you get trapped in this illusion, you will ultimately experience emptiness.

These are the five illusions of manhood that are perpetuated throughout our society. It is absolutely imperative that you recognize these illusions and not be trapped by them. A new conversation with men intends to assist you in breaking free from all of these illusions, so I would now like to share some concrete things you can do to break free from the illusions.

You must be willing to become aware that the illusion exists.

This is always the most difficult and challenging step, and at the same time, it is always the first step. As soon as you become aware that you are trapped in the illusion, you have already begun waking up from it. Take some time and reflect on these illusions and then write down the one that resonates the most for you. By writing down the illusion, it will begin to lose its grip on you. Imagine the illusion as internal darkness and your awareness as eternal light. By shining the light onto the darkness, the darkness disappears. Your awareness is the light that will remove the darkness. Challenge yourself to become aware of the illusion you may be caught in.

You must be willing to be transformed by the renewing of your mind.

This is what I mean by having a new conversation with men. It means becoming aware of old belief systems, thought patterns, and assumptions that are in your mind that may no longer be working for you. By changing your internal dialog (conversation), you lay the foundation for new ways of being a man. Think of your mind as a garden and all of your thoughts as seeds. Whatever seed (thought) you plant has to grow. If you are planting negative seeds, guess what grows? If you are planting positive seeds, what do you think will sprout up? Transforming your mind means that you make a conscious effort in recognizing what types of seeds you are planting. The more conscious you become the more likely you are to plant positive seeds. This also means that you become conscious of all of the things that you are allowing to be planted in your mind. This means that you should limit your exposure to all of the negative seeds that are planted by our media. So do yourself a favor and disconnect from too much television.

You must be willing to heal and reconnect to your emotions.

This is definitely our greatest challenge as men. As I mentioned, we are conditioned not to feel, but it is our responsibility to go against societal conditioning and become courageous enough to begin our emotional-healing process. Until you learn to heal and feel, there will always be something missing in your life. I will go into greater depth and detail about this in Chapter Five titled "Transformation."

You must seek support.

You must understand that you cannot do this alone. I understand how difficult it is for men to seek support, but the fact remains you must seek help. I don't care if you go to therapy, join a men's group, join AA, or go to a church group. It is important that you surround yourself with like-minded men who can support and challenge you to become the best man you can be. Gaining the courage to seek support is a surefire way to help you break free from any of these illusions. I highly recommend that you join our online community at www.anewconversationwithmen.com, because it is filled with resources designed to help you break free from these illusions, and it will put you in contact with other men who are on the same journey as you. They can serve as role models and mentors for you and help you recognize that you are never alone.

You must develop a spiritual connection that works for you.

This does not necessarily mean that you have to join a church or other religious organization. It means that you must come to your own understanding that there is a power greater than yourself in the universe. Connecting to this power will give you strength, faith, and courage to break free from the illusions and live a more rewarding and fulfilling life. Once you develop this connection, it is your responsibility to nurture it and insure that you stay connected to it.

So there you have them, the five illusions of manhood:

1. *To be a man, you must be non-emotional and disconnected.*
2. *To be a man, you must have status, positions and power.*
3. *To be a man, you must have money and material possessions.*

4. *To be a man, you must use sexual conquest as a gauge for manhood.*

5. *To be a man, you must win at all costs and compete against other men.*

And these are the five things you can do to wake up from the illusions:

1. *You must be willing to become aware that the illusion exists.*
2. *You must be willing to be transformed by the renewing of your mind.*
3. *You must be willing to heal and reconnect to your emotions.*
4. *You must seek support.*
5. *You must develop a spiritual connection that works for you.*

In order to make the world a better place, we must recognize these illusions and remove them from our collective psyches. It begins with each man waking up and choosing to break free from these illusions. In doing so, the world will be a much better place for everyone.

Are you willing to look at the man in the mirror and ask him to change his ways?

"The real accomplishment in life is the art of being a warrior, which is the only way to balance the terror of being a man with the wonder of being a man."

— Carlos Castaneda

Chapter Four

The Five Masks of Masculinity

During the early 1990s, I embarked on a journey of self-discovery that would eventually lead me to discovering who I am and why I am here. It had begun with my experience with therapy, and it evolved into my attending personal-development workshops, listening to hours upon hours of lectures, and literally reading hundreds of books dealing with psychology, philosophy, metaphysics, and spirituality.

As I look back, I realize that at the beginning, I never dreamed of becoming a writer or speaker. My intention was not to become some expert or guru; my intention was to simply find my joy and be happy with myself. I had given up on my external pursuit of wealth and material things and challenged myself to look within and go a lot deeper. I instinctively knew that life could be more fulfilling and meaningful, and I became willing to give up everything in order to find meaning and purpose in my life.

This twenty-year journey of self-exploration and discovery has yielded some amazing answers to some of life's most important questions for me. As a result of this journey, I have been rewarded with internal treasures that fill my heart with joy, peace, and contentment that goes well beyond intellectual understanding. I have discovered my purpose, and that purpose is to share what I have learned with others so that they too can discover who they really are.

That is the purpose of this book, to simply be a guide for you to discover who you are and why you are here.

I have come to the conclusion that life was meant to be good, but no one said that it would be easy. If you choose to take the road less traveled, then I can assure you that you will reap untold wealth and riches that have absolutely nothing to do with material and monetary possessions. But you must be willing to engage in a new conversation with yourself so that you can gain access to these riches. This is the key to your success. To enter into a conversation that helps you discover who you are and why you are here on this planet.

To assist you in this quest, I would like to share some more lessons I have learned that have helped me. As always, simply remain open-minded to see if the lessons resonate with you. If not, simply disregard the lesson, but stay engaged in the conversation.

As mentioned, back in the early 1990s, I was introduced to what was then called the "Men's Movement." The men's movement was about men coming together to openly and honestly discuss the unspoken fears and concerns as well as the joys and thrills of being a man. My understanding is that it really began after a gentleman by the name of Robert Bly wrote a book titled *Iron John.* His book was followed by *Fire in the Belly* by Sam Keen, and *In the Company of Men* by Marvin Allen. As a result of these books and subsequent speaking lectures around the country, the Men's Movement expanded, and a new paradigm of masculinity began to spread. In this new paradigm, men were learning the importance of breaking away from the antiquated ways of being a man, and they began embracing new more nurturing and compassionate ways of being men. Mr. Bly and several other prominent writers, psychologists, and clergy began spreading the message that it was okay for men to be in touch with their emotions, and they began holding workshops and lectures that not only talked about men reconnecting with their "feminine" side, but also provided them with processes to help them reconnect to their emotions.

As a result of this new shift in male thinking, several other organizations started introducing some of the concepts and philosophies that Mr. Bly and others had talked about, and after a couple of years, the men's movement had grown and was reaching thousands of men around the country. The organization that probably received the most media attention at the time was a Christian-based organization called Promise Keepers. Promise Keepers was based on biblical teachings, and it challenged men to take responsibility for their families and for their own personal well-being. Their primary focus was on winning men to Christ and challenging them to embrace seven promises that they believed would help men become better men. During the '90s, they would hold large rallies in sports stadiums around the country, and men from all walks of life would come in and commit to following the scriptures to become better men. Although I didn't agree with the religious exclusivity of PK, I believe it was (and still is) a wonderful organization that has done a great job of challenging men to be the best men that they possibly can be.

In addition to Promise Keepers, there was The Mankind Project. Here is a description of MKP which I copied from their website, www.mkp.org:

The ManKind Project® is a progressive men's organization striving to be increasingly inclusive and affirming of cultural differences, especially with respect to color, class, sexual orientation, faith, age, ability, ethnicity, and nationality.

The ManKind Project® offers trainings which support men in developing lives of integrity, accountability, and connection to feeling. Our trainings challenge men to develop their abilities as leaders, partners, fathers, and elders in order to offer their deepest gifts in service to the world. **The ManKind Project®** is an educational organization committed to empowering men to missions of service. Except for those organizations listed on this page [their web page], MKP endorses, supports, and associates with no other organizations, therapies, programs, agendas, or philosophies. Any organization suggesting any other purposes or outcomes on their websites (or in their literature) for MKP's trainings is acting without MKP's consent or approval.

The ManKind Project's New Warrior Training Adventure® is an intense, transformative men's initiation which invites men to forge a deep conscious connection between head and heart. The NWTA offers men a powerful, challenging opportunity to look at all aspects of their lives in a richly supportive environment. **The New Warrior Training Adventure®** is the gateway to the ManKind Project.

I am a very proud graduate of the New Warrior Training Adventure (July 2002), and I will definitely say that it falls into my top-ten list of greatest experiences of my life. As a matter of fact, this book is an extension of my participation in the training. Although I am no longer active, I still use the things I learned from the training in all areas of my life. One thing I learned was to always be in service to humanity by sharing my gifts and talents with the world and by fulfilling my personal mission. My personal mission in the training was "As a man amongst men, I create a world of love and understanding by loving myself and understanding others." I do my best to fulfill this mission and use it as a guidepost for my interaction with others on a day-to-day basis. I am truly grateful for the experience and the lessons I learned from this training.

These two organizations, Promise Keepers and The New Warrior Adventure, laid the foundation for a new shift in male consciousness around the country and throughout the world during the '90s. Unfortunately, there is very little media coverage today of these two organizations, and when there is coverage, it's usually negative. But I believe these types of organizations hold the keys to this country's success. When we can educate, motivate, and inspire men to be great husbands, fathers, lovers, and friends, we begin creating solutions to the multiplicity of challenges facing our world. My hope is that this book will reignite the fire of the men's movement and challenge men to embrace this new paradigm of masculinity.

During the 90s, there was a men's council and meeting place in Houston, Texas, in which I was an active participant. The council was composed of several graduates of the New Warrior Adventure as well as some nationally known leaders of the men's movement. Not only did I listen to and participate with some of the leading men in the movement, I also jump-started my speaking career by speaking at the council on several different occasions. I really enjoyed being a member of the council and discovered that I had a real passion and a talent for teaching and speaking about men's issues. Although

THE FIVE MASKS OF MASCULINITY

I was still relatively new to a lot of the psychological concepts and theories, I wanted to follow in the footsteps of the courageous men of the council, and that is why I continue to write and speak today. I am eternally grateful for the support and wisdom offered by these men, and my hope is that I can continue their work through this book and through my seminars and website.

Of all the things I learned at the council, I have to admit that learning about the five masks of masculinity was probably the most important. I'm not 100% sure, but I believe I learned this from nationally known therapist Marvin Allen, who I mentioned earlier. It's been approximately eighteen years since I attended this lecture, and though I'm questioning who I learned this from, the content is still fresh in my mind.

In this lecture, Mr. Allen talked about how men begin wearing psychological masks as a way to deal with their repressed emotions. His theory was that when we, as children, experience any type of physical and emotional trauma, our minds try to compensate by creating defense mechanisms to minimize the pain. As we begin to shut down our emotions, we begin to rely strictly on our intellects. In order to cope, we create these metaphoric masks, which then become our pseudo-identity. In other words, it isn't who we really are; it's our ego developing an alter ego. This alter ego then becomes our identity, and we begin playing out the roles from behind the masks.

The reason that I remember this lesson so vividly is because, at the time of the lesson, I was still wearing my metaphorical mask. I was trapped behind this mask and pretending to be someone that I wasn't, and as I listened to the lecture, I realized that I had to do whatever it took to remove my mask and become authentic. As a result of that lecture, I recommitted myself to discovering who I really was, and that was one of the things that propelled me to continue my journey of self-discovery and remove my mask of self-deception.

So now, I would like to share the five masks with you. As you read these, simply recognize that there is a small part of you that may be found in each of the masks. Try not to judge them as good or bad, right or wrong. Simply see them as artificial identities that you may have developed to protect yourself. The good news is that as soon as you become aware that you are wearing one, it begins to loosen its grip on you, and before you know it, you won't even be wearing it at all. But the key is to acknowledge that you may be wearing one so that you can then break through your denials.

As you read these, try to recognize which one resonates with you. I can assure you that if you are truly honest with yourself you will immediately recognize which one you may or may not be wearing. Just try to stay focused so that you connect with the one that is most appropriate for you. (The titles that Mr. Allen used were slightly different from the ones I am using here. I have modified them just a little for my own understanding and explanation.) Here are the five masks:

Mr. Nice Guy Mr. Tough as Nails Mr. Money Bags Mr. Gigolo Mr. Stuck in His Head

I would now like to give my interpretations and explanations of what these masks represent and how they can unconsciously affect our lives. It is important that you really take the time to recognize which one "fits" for you and then take the time to recognize and ultimately remove the mask. Just remember that this can be extremely challenging and confusing at first. But if you will take some time and contemplate the lessons in this chapter, it can serve as a springboard for your awakening and transformation. Remember, the first step in removing your mask is to simply become aware of which one you are wearing. By becoming aware, you open the door to transforming your life for the better, but you must be willing to walk through the door so that the masks are no longer necessary.

Mr. Nice Guy

As I listened to the facilitator speak about the Mr. Nice Guy mask, I was absolutely captivated by his presentation. Everything he said seemed to hit home for me, and I immediately recognized that this was the mask that I had been hiding behind all of my life.

As I reflected back on my life, I could see how wearing this mask had done two things. The first thing it had done was keep me from feeling and expressing my own real emotions. As a result of some physical and emotional trauma in my childhood, I learned to repress and shut down how I really felt. For example, instead of being able to express my anger, I would usually smile and pretend that I really wasn't mad. No matter how angry I felt inside, I would hold it in and pretend that the anger wasn't there. Before I knew it, I had completely lost my ability to feel and express anger. This had always been a real problem for me, yet I never recognized it until this lecture. As I thought about it deeply, I could see how hiding behind this mask had

had a very negative impact on my self-esteem and sense of self-worth. Because I was always denying my true feelings, I was constantly negating myself and putting other people's needs ahead of my own, which led to the second thing that wearing the mask had done to me.

The second thing it had done was cause me to become an incessant people pleaser. Since I had such a difficult time expressing my true feelings, it was impossible for me to really feel good about myself. To try to compensate for my feelings of inadequacy, I developed an insatiable need to please other people. This need to please became my Mr. Nice Guy mask, which I wore to not only get people to like me, but also to try to get them to love me. The sad part is that as long as I was wearing that mask, I could never experience their love. I had to be willing to remove my mask so that I could be myself and allow people to love me for me and not for the fake Mr. Nice Guy mask I was wearing.

These were just two of the things I learned during this lecture, and as a result, I spent the next ten years learning how to remove my mask and become comfortable with who I really am. It wasn't easy, but I can assure you that removing my mask was probably the greatest gift I have ever given myself.

As you're thinking about these masks, I must also inform you of the good news. The good news is that there is always a flip side to wearing a mask. As you become aware of your mask and begin to remove it, you will also begin to recognize that wearing the mask also brought you a gift. You may not be able to recognize the gifts at first, but I can assure you that they are there waiting to be discovered.

Here are just a few of the gifts I received as a result of wearing my Mr. Nice Guy mask:

Wearing my mask actually helped me become a more caring and compassionate person.

Wearing my mask challenged me to become a positive, optimistic person.

Wearing my mask challenged me to question things more deeply and become a lifelong student of learning.

Each person's experience will obviously be different, but as soon as you become willing to recognize that you have a mask on you, actually begin taking it off. So, to assist you in this process, I'd like to ask you a couple of questions if you think you may be wearing the Mr. Nice Guy mask:

Do you have difficulty expressing the emotion of anger? Are you constantly seeking other people's approval?

Do you always pretend that everything is all right even when it's not? Do you have difficulty accepting compliments?

Do you feel "stuck" in life?

Take a moment and ponder these questions. If you answered yes to any of them, then it's quite possible that you are trapped behind the Mr. Nice Guy mask. Spend a little time reflecting on your life and see if this mask resonates with you. I will discuss ways to remove the mask at the end of the next chapter. Let's move on to the next mask.

Mr. Tough as Nails

Have you ever met a man who seldom smiles and appears angry most of the time? Do you know of anyone who never shows any emotion except anger and negativity and flies into a rage over some of the most insignificant situations? Do you know anyone who never has a kind word to say about anything or anybody? Do you know of anyone who is always ready, willing, and able to start a fight for the smallest provocation?

If you do, then there is a very good chance that you know someone who is wearing the Mr. Tough as Nails mask. In a society that teaches men that they must be tough in order to be a man, it's no wonder so many men embrace this mask. This mask goes hand in hand with the first illusion of manhood which I discussed in the previous chapter. The first illusion was, *"To be a man, you must be non-emotional and disconnected."*

When a man wears this mask, he loses his ability to experience positive emotions. As a matter of fact, he will do everything in his power never to show emotion. The only emotion he is comfortable with is anger or rage, and therefore, it is usually the only emotion he will express. The sad part is that he usually has a heart of gold beneath his rage, yet he does not know how to connect to it. His defense mechanism of anger sometimes covers up his deep feelings of sadness and fear, so he uses his anger to feel a false sense of power and control. Mr. Tough as Nails can be controlling and manipulative, and he will deny his true feelings by creating a wall of anger and non-attachment. If you feel that this is the mask you may be wearing, ask yourself these questions:

Do you get angry easily?

Do you have difficulty smiling and feeling happy?

Do you rationalize your anger by saying that is just the way men are? Do you notice that your body is usually tense and constricted?

Do you judge men who can verbally express their emotions as being weak, soft or sissies?

Remember that the key to removing your mask is to simply become aware that you have one. Simply take some time to see if you recognize yourself wearing either of these masks. It is extremely important that you pay attention to your body as you're reading this. Try and notice any physical discomfort inside of you. If reading this triggers anything inside of you, then that means that you are definitely on the right track to identifying with the mask you may be wearing. Try to recognize the feeling within and just let it move through you.

Mr. Money Bags

This mask is a direct result of the third illusion of manhood, which is, *To be a man, you must have money and material possessions.* You will recognize Mr. Money Bags by his attachment to material things. He is the guy that is always trying to impress you with his "stuff." It could be his car or clothes or jewelry, or maybe his bank account. No matter which one it is, he is always making sure that you see his "stuff." This is the same guy who will try to impress a woman by spending an insane amount of money on a first date with a woman who he doesn't even know yet. This is really his way of saying, "I know you won't like me for who I am, so instead, I will try to 'buy' your love for me."

What he doesn't realize is that his need to impress people is driven by his mask. And as long as he wears the mask, no amount of money will ever fill the emptiness he feels inside. If you feel connected to this mask, ask yourself these questions:

Do you brag about your "stuff" to others?

Are you always trying to keep up with the Joneses?

Are you constantly lending money to friends that never pay you back?

Are your credit cards maxed out because of excessive spending?

Do you spend unnecessary amounts of money on things to try to impress others?

Do you relate to this mask? Let it sink in as we move on to the next one.

Mr. Gigolo

Remember illusion number four? *To be a man, you must use sexual conquest as a gauge for manhood.* This is the foundation of Mr. Gigolo's behavior. Mr. Gigolo is so caught up in this illusion that he always justifies his actions by asserting what a "man" he is whenever he has sex. This is one of the reasons why some men brag about impregnating women without having any intention of being a father. Getting a woman pregnant is a way of a man's saying that he has sexual power, and it temporarily inflates his already deflated ego.

A man who is trapped behind this mask will constantly seek validation by having sex with as many women as possible.

Unfortunately, his behavior is driven by a deep sense of inadequacy, and no matter how many women he sleeps with, his insecurities still remain. Each conquest gives him a temporary high that is short-lived because it is based only on the physical aspect of sex. What he does not realize is that what he really craves is emotional intimacy and connection; unfortunately, his mask will not allow him to have that which he so desperately craves. All sexual addictions are driven by this mask. If this mask is not removed, it becomes impossible for a man to create loving, connected, monogamous relationships. No matter how much a woman may love a man, and no matter what she may do to satisfy him sexually, if a man is trapped behind this mask, he will constantly seek sexual conquest in many different forms. These include but are not limited to pornography, infidelity, and even child molestation.

In our sex-crazed culture, this mask is becoming more and more widespread, and men are beginning to exhibit this negative behavior at earlier ages than ever. If you feel you may be trapped behind this particular mask, ask yourself these questions:

Do you feel a "letdown" after sex?

Do you find yourself addicted to pornography?

Do you spend time in strip clubs without telling your spouse? Are you obsessed with sex and are never truly satisfied with it? Do you demand sex from your spouse even when she says no?

It takes an incredible amount of courage to answer these questions honestly. I hope you take the time to contemplate these questions and see if you identify with this particular mask. If so, just remember that the simple recognition of the mask begins the process of removing it.

Our final mask is:

Mr. Stuck in His Head

I once had a personal coaching session with a very beautiful woman who complained about her husband's lack of emotional availability. Her complaint was that he did not show affection, and he was obsessively controlling. She said that he happened to be an engineer and that it was important to him to analyze everything she did. He had a Ph.D., and he made sure that everyone knew it, especially her.

As she sat there crying, she shared how he was extremely anal about everything and always wanted to "intellectualize" her actions. He would quote case studies and technical journals about why men and women behave the way they did and he always spoke to her as though he was her professor instead of her mate. He was very good at reciting statistics and theories, but he could not speak openly about his feelings or share how he actually felt about her.

After a year or so of counseling (with a therapist), they divorced. I coached her for approximately six months after her divorce and she eventually moved on with her life to another city.

A year or so later, I was giving a talk at the men's council and I was speaking on why it's so difficult for men to express their feelings. I talked about the importance of getting out of our heads and into our hearts and I shared some of my personal struggles with this issue.

I talked about the phenomenon of being "stuck in the head," and it really got a lot of men's attention. Apparently, there were a lot of men who had experienced this, and they were definitely relating to my talk.

After my talk, a man walked up to me and told me just how much he enjoyed it. He said that he really related to my story because he had always had difficulty expressing his feelings. He said he wished he would have heard the talk a few years earlier because his being "stuck in his head" had caused him to lose his marriage. He said that maybe if he had heard the talk back then, he would not have lost the woman that he truly loved and cared about. After a few moments of conversing, we eventually started to talk about his ex-wife, and it turned out that she was the woman that I had been coaching a couple of years earlier.

I never told him about my sessions with his ex-wife, but I did tell him that it was possible for him to create a new love affair as long as he was willing to get out of his head and into his heart. He definitely agreed and told me that he was committed to doing just that.

Mr. Stuck in His Head is probably the least recognizable of all the masks. Most of us as men probably analyze things too much, but that does not mean that we are wearing this particular mask. If you think you may be wearing this mask, ask yourself these questions:

Are you able to express how you feel versus what you think? Can you make the distinction between the two?

Has anyone ever told you that you think too much in relationships?

Are you an accountant, engineer, or mathematician who gets lost in numbers and statistics?

Do you have difficulty having fun and laughing out loud?

Spend some time with these questions and see if they resonate with you. If you feel that you are stuck in your head, it's important that you get out of your head and into your heart if you ever want to feel fully alive.

So there you have them, the Five Masks of Masculinity:

Mr. Nice Guy Mr. Tough as Nails Mr. Money Bags Mr. Gigolo Mr. Stuck in His Head

Did you relate to any of them? Do you already know which is your strong suit? If you recognize which is the one you are wearing, are you willing to take it off? Are you willing to do whatever it takes to remove the mask and become the authentic male that you were destined to be?

If the answer is yes, then the first thing you must do is embrace *A New Conversation with Men*. This simply means that you become willing to see yourself from a different point of view. This new conversation will allow you to become open-minded to change which opens the door to your transformation. The next thing you must be willing to do is heal your heart. This is the key that unlocks the door to removing your masks. It is probably the most important and at the same time the most difficult thing you must do. But it is the only way through for you. If you've come this far in the book, then I already know that you're ready, so let's move to the next chapter, which will provide you with some specific tools to remove your masks and create the life you deserve.

The next chapter is transformation and it holds the keys to your empowerment and enlightenment. Let's get started.

"And do not be conformed to this world, but be transformed by the renewing of your mind, so that you may prove what the will of God is, that which is good and acceptable and perfect."

— Romans 12:2

Chapter Five
Transformation

Are you willing to break free from the Five Illusions of Manhood that will only cause pain and suffering in your life? Are you tired of wearing the Five Masks of Masculinity I spoke about in the previous chapter? I can assure you that the only way you will wake up from the illusions and remove your masks is to discover who you really are. I can assure you that it is definitely possible to create a life filled with great relationships, vibrant health, financial abundance, a fulfilling career, and a spiritual connection that truly nurtures your soul. In other words, you can have it all, but there is one thing you must be willing to do. You must engage in your own personal transformation. This is something you must commit to and stick to. It is the key that unlocks every door and fulfills every dream. It is the journey of transformation, and it should actually be a lifelong process. I must make a distinction here between motivation and transformation because they aren't necessarily the same thing. Motivation is what occurs when someone says something that "motivates" you to do something you would not ordinarily have done. If you go to a motivational seminar the speaker's job is to "motivate" you to take action. The downside of motivation is that it is most often temporary. As soon as the "motivator" is gone, so too is the motivation. After a few days or weeks, then the person who was "motivated" reverts right back to their old behaviors and patterns.

On the other hand, transformation is a permanent process. If you truly engage in this process, then your behaviors do not revert back to the old ways of behaving.

The Encarta World English Dictionary defines transformation as:

1. "a complete change, usually into something with an improved appearance or usefulness. 2. the act or process of transforming somebody or something."

I will define transformation as "the process in which you discover your unconscious thoughts, feelings, and beliefs and then make a conscious effort to change them if needed." When you are able to change your thoughts, feelings, and beliefs, then you will experience transformation. When you engage in true transformation, I can assure you that you do not revert back to old behaviors.

In order to do this, you must remember this adage: "If you don't go within, you will always go without." This means that you must look deep within yourself to discover any hidden beliefs that may be sabotaging your life. It is only through this transformational process that you can uncover and then change your beliefs, which will then assist you in changing your life.

Before I engage in an explanation of transformation I want to share a very important story with you. This story contains a universal truth, that when fully comprehended, will lay the foundation for your personal transformation. As you read the story, listen with an open heart and an open mind. Be receptive to the powerful message that it contains.

One day, God was sitting in heaven watching over His divine creations called human beings. As He watched over them, He recognized that although there were a few who acted out in negative ways, the vast majority of them were loving, caring and compassionate beings. As He watched over them with love and admiration, He decided that He wanted to do something special, something that He had never done before. So He called His angels together and came up with a plan to give the humans a very special gift.

God: *I have decided that I want to give human beings something very special. I want to give them divinity. I want to give them a part of Me. With this gift, they will be able to co-create with Me and create anything their heart desires. It is a divine gift that I think they really deserve. But I do not want to just give it to them. I want them to earn it. I want them to put forth some effort to find this very special gift. The reason I have brought you together is that I need you to help me figure out where to put it. Where can I place this gift that makes it difficult but not impossible to find? Where in the world should a gift of this importance be placed?*

After a few moments of silence, one of the angels spoke.

Angel 1: *I know a good place. Why not place Your gift on top of the highest mountain?*

God: *I have given human beings the gift of courage and strength, surely they would have no problem climbing a mountain and finding this gift. I believe that would be too easy.*

Angel 2: *How about placing it beneath the sea? Surely they would not think to look there.*

TRANSFORMATION

God: *I have given them knowledge and persistence. If they can scale mountains, I'm sure that it would not be difficult for them to get to the bottom of the sea. I believe that would still be too easy.*

Angel 3: *I know a place. Why not place your gift amongst the stars?*

Surely that would be a difficult place for them to look.

God: *"When they combine their courage and strength with knowledge and persistence, I do not believe they would have a difficult time finding my gifts among the stars. Although these are all very good ideas, I still do not believe that we have found the perfect place. There has to be another place that we have not thought of yet."*

Suddenly, another angel stepped up and said:

Angel 4: *"I believe I know the perfect place. I believe this would be the very last place that humans would look. Although it seems easy, I think humans would have an extremely difficult time looking for your gift in this perfect place. It may appear to be simple, but I believe it would be the greatest challenge ever put forth for them. Why not place your very special gift inside of them? Why not place it in their hearts? It would be so close but yet so far because I believe it would be the very last place that they would ever think to look. Your gift of divinity should be placed within them."* For a brief moment, God sat in silence. Then He smiled as only a joyful

God could smile and embraced the angel.

God: *"You are absolutely right. This would be the perfect place for My gift. Thank all of you for your suggestions, but without question, this will be the perfect place to put it. From this day forward, a divine spark of Me will be placed within the heart of every human being, thereby giving them My greatest gift, the gift of co-creation. With this gift, all humans will now be able to create anything that their hearts desire. Let it be so!"*

I share that story because I think it provides a divine truth. I personally believe that we really do have this divine gift within us, and it is our responsibility to access it. It does not matter if you believe in God or not. You simply must be willing to look within yourself and locate your special gift. My hope is that this book will be a guide to help you find that gift. In this chapter, I would like to share my own story of transformation and then provide some insights on how you, too, can be transformed.

As mentioned in the previous chapters, it wasn't until my divorce that I realized that there were some emotional and psychological issues that I was definitely afraid to address. Like most men, I was in complete denial that there was anything wrong with me. The time had come for me to face my demons head-on, and I had reached a point where I was either going to get help, or I was going to die. As a result of all the challenges I had been dealing with, I had begun having fleeting thoughts of suicide as a way to try to alleviate the pain I was in. This was a sure sign that I was in trouble, and I definitely needed help.

My first step to transformation began with my willingness to go see a therapist. I realize that there is a negative stigma amongst men associated with seeking help, and that is the reason I want to share my story. As men, we must be willing to change our conversation about what it means to be a man. Recognizing that we all need support at times is critical to a man's transformation. I hope that by sharing my story you may decide to take the first step to your own transformation if needed.

Going to therapy was probably the most difficult thing I had ever done up to that point in my life. Although I intuitively knew I needed to go, there was a part of me that was absolutely terrified. Some of the things that scared me the most were not knowing what to expect, not knowing how long it would take to "fix" me, and worrying about what people would think of me. I also had a fear that maybe something might really be wrong with me that I could not fix. I had always put on this in-control, got-it-all- together type persona, but the truth was, I was unraveling inside very rapidly, and I felt out of control and was scared to death.

What if I couldn't change? What if the therapy didn't work? Would the therapist really be able to understand me and my issues? And if so, would she be able to help me? So many questions, so few answers. These were just a few of the challenging fears that came up for me when I decided to get help. Eventually, I worked through these fears and took the steps necessary to begin my journey of transformation.

It's possible that you, the reader, may be faced with some of these same questions. My hope is that you will take the time to really listen to my story. As you read it, simply notice any feelings or thoughts that come up for you. If you resonate with what I've written, then follow the advice given.

Therapy

I remember locating a therapist in the phone book and then driving to her office and not having the courage to walk inside. I would pull into the parking lot and sit in my car and then talk myself out of going in. It took me approximately six visits before I actually walked inside the building and then another three tries before I gathered up the courage to actually go into her office. Once I did go in, my transformation had begun. Although it wasn't easy, I had taken the first step and was on my way to improving my life for the better. It is difficult to put in words but the old cliché of feeling as if a huge weight had been lifted from my shoulders is exactly how I felt. By being courageous enough to confront my fears, I opened the door to a brand new chapter of my life. I was now on the road to recovery, and it would lead me to places I could have never dreamed possible.

Going to therapy opened up a whole new world for me. Instead of focusing only on my intellect, I begin to learn how to connect to my heart. I was no longer concerned with making money and accumulating material things; I was now focusing all of my attention on simply learning how to be authentically happy. I was learning to understand who I was and how all the events of my life, beginning at childhood had shaped me into the man that I had become.

The first thing that I learned in therapy was that I had completely disconnected from my emotions. As the result of a pretty traumatic childhood, I had devised some pretty amazing defense mechanisms to keep me from feeling my feelings. One of those mechanisms was being nice. By being nice, I would always put other people's feelings ahead of my own. This is also called co-dependence. Co-dependence occurs when you are more concerned about other people's feelings than your own. It is usually driven by the fear that people will not like you if you express your own feelings authentically. By always being nice, I completely shut down the rest of my feelings, especially the feeling of anger. There was a part of me that thought that if I allowed myself to feel the anger I would go into an uncontrollable rage, so to avoid that, I would simply shut down all anger. This really destroyed my self-esteem and was the root cause of a lot of feelings of unhappiness I felt. It was really at the core of my depression and sadness. As I progressed through my transformation, I learned how to express my anger appropriately and to express my feelings authentically. In doing so, I began to reconnect with all of my emotions which was the key to my transformation.

Another important thing that I learned as a result of therapy was that I had a deep aversion to groups. Although I had no trouble speaking in front of groups of people at work, I was extremely uncomfortable speaking in a group about any personal issues. The reason for this was my deep fear of intimacy. Intimacy is experienced when you are able to feel your emotions and speak openly about them. Instead of speaking from my heart, I would always speak from my intellect, which is not the same. Whenever I would speak about work-related topics, there was no emotion involved because I was simply sharing information; therefore, there was no fear. But when it came to speaking from my heart and sharing my feelings, there was definitely a lot of fear. By facing the fear and moving directly through it, I eventually learned how to share myself openly and honestly with other people. I overcame my fear of intimacy by being willing to express my feelings without being afraid that the people I shared them with would judge or reject me. I had to be confident and secure enough in who I was to simply speak my truth without worrying about how other people felt or thought about me. This was definitely a liberating experience. It was the truth that set me free, and it set the stage for my commitment to discovering who I really was and what my purpose in life was.

Although this is a brief overview of my experience with therapy, it should give you some insights into the things I learned as a result of my participation. As you read through the remaining chapters of this book, you will have an opportunity to learn more about healing your own heart and discovering who you really are. My therapy was definitely the foundation of my transformation. It helped me heal my heart and transform my mind. This may or may not be for you, but I needed to share this experience because this is how my transformation began. If you feel moved to try therapy, by all means, do so. If you do not, there will be other opportunities for you to engage in throughout this book. As always, trust that still small voice within. Listen to your heart, and let it be your guide.

Although my therapy helped me heal a lot of the emotional and psychological scars I had been in denial about, I still refer to it as one of many doors I would eventually have to walk through. In addition to therapy, I participated in hundreds of hours of personal-development seminars. I have also read hundreds of books and listened to hundreds of hours of lectures pertaining to human potential and personal growth. All of these activities were simply doors that I chose to walk through to become a better man. Remember, this book is simply a door. If you choose to walk through it, be prepared to be transformed for the better.

As you read this book, I want you to understand that my story is also your story. The fact of the matter is that all men are created equal. We all have joys and pains, successes and failures, fear and courage, in addition to hopelessness and faith. In the words of Dr. King, "We

TRANSFORMATION

are all tied together in a single garment of destiny." Our mission is to figure out how to weave our stories into this divine garment called life.

So the next questions you must ask yourself are these: "Are you willing to weave your own personal story of triumph into life?" Are you man enough to join *A New Conversation with Men* and help create a new paradigm of masculinity?"

If you answered yes, then I believe you are ready to be transformed. As a matter of fact, if you have read this far into the book already, then I know that you are already committed to your own transformation. The truth of the matter is that most men are not ready to begin this journey. Most men are so trapped in the old paradigm of masculinity that they would never begin the process. As mentioned in the previous chapters, most men are still sleepwalking through life and would rather remain asleep than become awake. Waking up is extremely difficult, but it is the only way that a man can truly find himself and discover his purpose and passion in life.

In order to begin the process of transformation, I believe it is absolutely imperative that you take a life inventory. The purpose of the inventory is to simply make you aware of areas in your life that can possibly be improved. Once you take the inventory, it gives you a good starting point to begin your own transformational process.

Here is how it works. Below, you will find seven categories of your life that are critical to your success and happiness. The first step is to simply grade these seven areas of your life on a scale of 1 to 10, ten being the highest and best score. Take just a moment and rate these seven areas.

Your personal relationships. (Rate your marriage, best friends, boyfriends, girlfriends, children etc.) Score____

Your intellectual growth. (Do you like to read and learn new things?) Score___

Your health (Do you smoke? Are you overweight? Do you abuse drugs?) Score____

Your finances (Are you robbing Peter to pay Paul?) Score _____

Your emotional awareness (Are you comfortable expressing your feelings? Can you honestly identify them? Are you happy with your life?) Score

Your spirituality (Do you have a spiritual connection or practice?) Score

Your sense of purpose (Do you believe your life has a purpose?) Score

As you are rating these categories, pay close attention to your thoughts and feelings. Simply notice what comes up for you as you rate your life. This is not a scientific survey or process. It is simply an opportunity to focus your awareness on your current life situation. A lot of men are so focused on their jobs and accumulating material things that they refuse to ask themselves deeper questions. How about you? Are you willing to go within so that you do not have to go without? If you refuse to take the time to fill this out, what does that say about you? It simply says that maybe you are not ready to begin your journey of transformation. Maybe you would rather stay stuck in your old ways of being a man. Obviously, that is your choice, but I would like to suggest that you reconsider. Hopefully, you are reading this book to gain insights to assist you in improving the quality of your life, and if so, here is your opportunity to truly engage in your personal transformation.

Is there a part of you that is saying, this is silly and irrelevant? Have you already convinced yourself that your life is fine, and there is no reason for you to do the exercise? Are you rationalizing and analyzing what it all means and judging yourself based on your score? Have you already decided that you simply refuse to do this?

No matter what you have decided to do about this exercise, I'd like to share a simple yet powerful quote with you. "If you keep doing what you've been doing, you'll keep getting what you've always got." Didn't you start reading this book because you believed there was some valuable information in it to help you improve the quality of your life? Are you really committed to yourself and your transformation? Well, here is a great starting point to see just how committed you are. Be sure to complete the exercise, and I can assure you that you are actively participating in your personal transformation.

Now let's take a look at your score. How did you do? Are you surprised by any of your scores? Which areas of your life scored the lowest? How about the highest? If you didn't score 70 points, what can you do to improve your score? The keys to your happiness lie within your willingness to examine these areas and then commit to improving them. But remember, "If you don't go within, you will always go without," which means, if you don't participate in your own transformation, you will go without having dynamic health, great relationships, financial abundance, a fulfilling career, and a spiritual connection that truly nurtures your soul. Transformation is the process of going within. Are you willing to engage in this process?

Unfortunately, most men will wait until they are in a deep, severe crisis before they will begin the process of transformation. Most of us wait until we have ended a relationship or are caught in the middle of a divorce or maybe have lost our job before we realize that something needs to change within us. Sometimes we are swimming in debt or possibly dealing with health issues before we decide to make changes in our lives. I want you to know that all of these events are simply wake-up calls that are designed to help you begin your transformational journey. My intention in this book is to help minimize the challenges and discomfort you experience and help you along the way to a better life. Just remember that you are not alone, and there are literally millions of men who are going through the exact same things that you are going through; men just like you who are hungry and waiting for *A New Conversation with Men*.

Before we get into some concrete things you can do to transform your life, I'd like to share five reasons men do not engage in this transformational process. Study these five things carefully and do not let them keep you from transforming your life.

The first thing that keeps men from participating in this process is fear. I know that sounds simple, but it is the foundation of all resistance. If you have ever wondered what is keeping you from reaching your full potential, I can assure you that fear is always at the core of it. Most of us as men believe that fear is a bad thing. Therefore we deny it and repress it by simply pretending it does not exist. Unfortunately, too many men become paralyzed by their fear and then find creative ways to deny that they are even afraid. This denial keeps us from taking action at an unconscious level. The secret is to simply feel the fear and do it anyway.

The second thing that keeps men from transforming their lives is emotional pain. Unfortunately, most of us do not even recognize that we are in emotional pain because we have been socially conditioned not to truly feel our emotions. In order to avoid feeling our pain, we anesthetize ourselves with things like drugs, work, sex, and alcohol to try to minimize the pain or not feel it at all. This is why so many of us are trapped in denial. We refuse to allow ourselves the opportunity to feel what's really going on in our hearts. It's important to understand that just because we don't feel something does not mean that it does not hurt or is not causing some type of emotional damage. It is this unconscious pain that causes so much dysfunction in our lives. Most of the pain we have is the result of unresolved emotional conflict from our past. Some of this pain is the result of our childhood, while some of it is simply the result of living as a man in today's society.

The third thing that keeps men from transforming their lives is the fear of being perceived as weak. Most men will do anything to maintain their image of being tough, strong, and in control. This is probably the greatest detriment to a man's well-being. This is the reason it is so difficult for men to ask for help. They simply are too afraid of what other people think and how they are perceived as men.

The forth thing that keeps men from transforming their lives is their need to be right. Most men would rather be right than happy. Men are notorious for taking firm positions against things, and they would rather give their lives about these positions than change them or simply admit that they are wrong. This very rigid need to be right will always keep men from being transformed. In addition to needing to be right, most men also struggle with simply saying, "I don't know." Somehow men have concluded that they are supposed to know everything (which is impossible) and they will do anything to try to project this image of being a know-it-all.

The fifth thing that keeps men from transforming their lives is their inability to see the benefit of emotional and spiritual transformation. As men, we generally process things on an intellectual level. For example, if I tell you that I can show you how to make a million dollars by taking a course in real estate, it's easy for a man to see the benefit of taking that course. In his intellect, he is able to make the connection between taking the course and making a million dollars. On the other hand, if I tell a man that he will experience joy, serenity and inner peace as a result of taking a transformational course, it's difficult, if not impossible for him to understand that benefit. The reason is, the benefit cannot be grasped by the intellect. It can only be experienced in the heart. Most men are so disconnected from their hearts that they cannot see the benefit of experiencing emotional and spiritual transformation.

These are the five things that keep men from transforming their lives. Did you relate to any of them? Which one did you identify with the most? Are you willing to move past these issues and be transformed? I'd like to share some things you can do to help you move through these five obstacles to your transformation.

You must recognize and accept the fact that fear is neither good nor bad, right or wrong. Fear is simply an emotion that is designed to keep you safe. It is an asset to your well-being, not a liability. Your goal should be to learn to recognize your fears so that you can gain the courage to move through them. The only way out of fear is directly through it, so you must not deny its existence. Learning to recognize, and most importantly, express your fears is a sign of strength, not a sign of weakness. You must learn to connect to your emotions. Learning to feel and express those feelings is probably the most important part of your transformation. Becoming aware of your basic human emotions (I'll discuss these in detail in a moment) is essential to creating and maintaining a rewarding and fulfilling life. Becoming aware of the sources of your pain gives you the impetus to remove that pain. What you can feel you can heal.

Transforming your life is definitely not a weakness. It will take every ounce of your courage and strength to engage in this process. You do not have to be tough and detached to be a man. Although some men may judge and criticize you for taking on this challenge, I can assure you that the rewards and benefits you will receive from your participation will be price-less. But you must accept the fact that you cannot do it alone. You must be willing to seek support in whatever form you need.

You must be willing to relinquish the need to be right. Letting go of your attachment to being right is essential to your transformation. It is perhaps your greatest challenge. It falls into the category of "simple but not easy." Letting go and surrendering is not the same as giving up and giving in. In addition to this, you must also be willing to simply say, "I don't know." It's okay not to know everything. It does not make you less of a man by saying you don't know something.

There is no way I can put into words the benefit of transformation. Words do not come close to the joy and gratitude I feel daily as a result of my own transformation. So I'm simply going to ask you to trust me. Trust me that you, too, can experience joy, gratitude, and inner peace. It is already in you. You simply have to commit to your transformation and let it all out.

So are you ready to be transformed? Are you ready, willing, and able to engage in the process? As always, the choice is up to you. What will you choose?

I would now like to share what I believe to be the three steps to permanent everlasting transformation. I have come to this conclusion as a result of my own twenty-year process. As stated earlier, I am not an expert or a doctor. I did not go to college or receive any type of psychology degree to come to these conclusions. I have come to these conclusions because I have lived through these challenges. I have personal, first-hand knowledge that these steps work because I have lived them, not just studied and formed theories about them. My knowledge comes from my experience, and that is exactly what I am sharing with you: my own experience. So as you read this, just listen with an open heart and an open mind and see if any of it resonates with you. Try not to judge or criticize what you read, simply ask yourself if it is applicable to you and your life. If so, simply follow the advice given. If not, simply move on to something else.

Step 1

The first step to permanent transformation is to heal your heart. I know that most men will reject this notion, but based on my experience, it is the foundation of personal transformation. Healing our heart means that we learn to connect with and express our feelings. There are basically four primary feelings that we have as human beings. They are, mad, sad, glad, and afraid. These feelings are the language of your soul. They are your internal guidance systems that help you navigate through life. Every other feeling you have is actually just a derivative of or a combination of one or more of these four feelings. For example, when a person says they feel jealous, what it possibly means is that they are feeling either mad, sad, afraid, or a combination of the three. Here is an example: Let's say you see your wife talking to another man. Some men would say that they feel jealous. But if they were willing to look a little deeper, they might come to the awareness that when they see their wife with another man, they possibly feel the energy of anger combined with the energy of sadness. The anger may come as a result of perceived betrayal, while the sadness may be a result of the possibility of losing someone you care about. The point is that the initial energy felt in the body is one or more of the four primary emotions. Emotions are simply energy in motion. There is no energy in the body called "jealous." Jealous is actually a thought that triggers one or more of the primary feelings.

The reason healing your heart is so important is that it teaches you to recognize and make distinctions about your emotions. It also helps you release any pain or hurt from the past that may be sabotaging your current relationships. Although you may not be aware of it, if you have unresolved emotional conflict, it will keep you from truly experiencing who you really are, and it will make it extremely difficult to create and maintain healthy fulfilling relationships.

Here is another way to look at it. Have you ever noticed how a child is able to feel and express emotions effortlessly? If a child feels joy, he laughs and smiles. If he feels sadness, he will cry. Kids don't think about emotions; they simply feel them and express them. They intuitively know how to express the energy that is moving through them. What's important to recognize about this is how a child feels emotions and then expresses them, and they then simply let go of that emotion. They do not hold onto emotional energy; they allow it to flow through them. A child can be extremely angry at a friend and throw a temper tantrum in one moment, and in the next moment, they are happy and joyful and hugging without any residual effects of the emotion of anger. This is how we are supposed to express our feelings. Unfortunately, as men, we are conditioned from a very young age to disconnect from our emotions. Through family and societal conditioning, we learn to start repressing and denying our feelings, which sets us up for emotional disconnection. Eventually, we lose the ability to feel, and we then begin processing everything through our intellect. In my opinion, this is the source of all of our addictive behaviors. When a man loses the ability to connect to his emotions, he begins to over-analyze and stay stuck in his head. His unresolved emotional conflict causes him to "think" instead of feel, and that is the source of a lot of his pain and suffering.

I believe this is why so many relationships fail: as men, we do not know how to connect to our hearts and express our very basic emotional needs. This disconnection keeps us from truly being "relational" in our relationships, and that is why they fail.

Think of your heart as a balloon. Every time you feel an emotion, the balloon fills up with air. When you allow yourself to simply feel the emotion and then express that emotion, it's like exhaling the air from the balloon. If you are emotionally healthy, you are able to feel the emotion (fill the balloon) and then express your feelings appropriately (release the air). This inhaling and exhaling keep the heart healthy and functioning properly. But, if every time you feel an emotion, you keep it bottled up inside of you without releasing it, your heart begins to build up pressure. Eventually, the pressure becomes so great that something has to happen so the balloon pops. This popping of the balloon causes men to act out in violent and inappropriate ways.

Think of why men act out so violently during road rage. Do you really believe that the person is really angry simply because they were cut off on the highway? I believe the reason some men act out this way is that they have all of this pent-up anger and sadness inside of them, and they do not know how to release it. So when they encounter someone who they perceive to be the source of their anger, they simply lash out in the way that they are accustomed to. Their balloon pops, and it is expressed through senseless acts of violence.

This is not only expressed through road rage. Whenever you see stories of domestic violence or child abuse, the same principle applies. A man has not been taught to heal his heart, and he is walking around with all of this pent-up, negative energy. The only way he knows how to deal with it is by striking out with violence. By teaching a man to heal his heart, we can minimize or eliminate these violent acts. When our country accepts this fact, I can assure you that we will begin seeing a reduction in our prison population and an overall reduction in senseless acts of violence. But in order to do this, we must begin *A New Conversation with Men*. In this new conversation, we will accept the fact that only a hurt person will hurt another person. We must get men to answer the challenging question, "What is it that hurts you so badly that you feel you must hurt someone else to heal it?"

We must encourage men to heal their hurts so that they will stop hurting each other. By engaging them in their emotional transformation, we lay the foundation for the eradication of a large percentage of the social ills that currently plague our world.

Emotional healing is the process one must go through if they are truly committed to their transformation. Remember what I said about the distinction between motivation and transformation? Motivation can be temporary, but transformation is permanent. If you commit to your emotional healing, I can promise you that your transformation will stay with you for the rest of your life. Heal your heart; transform your life!

Step 2

The next step to permanent transformation is the constant expansion of your mind and intellect. Although most people who go to college tend to stop learning once they graduate, I believe that learning is a lifelong process that each of us must engage in. If you are truly committed to your transformation, you must recognize that your mind is like a muscle. It simply gets stronger the more you use it. Make sure you exercise this muscle by reading books, participating in seminars, listening to intellectually stimulating programs, and taking courses to learn new things. Studies have shown that people who regularly engage their minds are far less likely to develop Alzheimer's disease in their later years. My suggestion is that you commit to learning something outside of your field of expertise. Remember in the first chapter where I talked about my love for business books? All I used to read were books on making money and getting rich. But it wasn't until I started reading personal growth and spirituality books that my real transformation began. Follow my example. If you're the type of person that never reads self-help books, here is an opportunity for you to expand your mind. If you're the type of person that only reads self-help books, take a break and read a book about your financial health. It's all about getting out of your comfort zone and trying something different.

Expanding your mind and intellect also means challenging your long-held beliefs and points of view. If you've never interacted with someone of a different race, now would be a good time to take that on. If you're the type of person that sees the glass as half empty, find an optimist who sees the glass as half full and engage in some dialog with him. Listen with an open mind, and challenge yourself to see things from a different point of view. But most importantly, make sure that you commit to discovering who you really are. This is an inside job, and it is the most important decision you will ever make. Discovering who you really are is the reason you are here. It is your sole responsibility as a human being. If you are successful in this endeavor, I can assure you that everything else will pale in comparison. Discovering who you really are is the Holy Grail of your existence. Be sure to make it your priority by expanding your mind and challenging your intellect.

Step 3

The third step to permanent transformation is to develop a spiritual connection with something greater than yourself. As a former atheist,

I completely understand if you are skeptical about this step. On the other hand, I also know there are those of you who completely agree with me. The fact of the matter is that you must find your own truth when it comes to spirituality. I will go into greater detail in Chapter 9, but I believe that this is probably the most important of the three steps to transformation. When I say, "Develop a spiritual connection," I am not asking you to accept any religious dogma or doctrine. I'm not asking you to go to church or to be "converted." I'm simply asking you to be open-minded to the possibility that there is a power greater than yourself in the universe. Some people call this power God, Yahweh, Jehovah, Great Spirit, Jesus, Buddha, Krishna or Mohammed. I do not believe that the name you use is that important. I do, however, believe that it is of the utmost importance that you develop a relationship with it no matter what name you use.

So there you have it. The three steps to permanent transformation:

Step 1. Heal your heart.

Step 2. Expand your mind and intellect.

Step 3. Develop a spiritual connection with something greater than yourself.

I would now like to share some steps I've taken to assist me in engaging and maintaining my personal transformation. I want you to understand that the things I am about to share have worked for me. There is no guarantee that they will work for you. As always, trust your own inner wisdom as you read my suggestions. Each human being is unique. You must accept your uniqueness and be willing to act on any impulse that you feel. If it feels right to you, heed the suggestions.

Healing My Heart

As I've mentioned, I have spent the last twenty years fully engaged in my own transformation. If I were to choose the one thing that had the most impact on healing my heart, it would have to be inner-child work. Inner child work allowed me to get to the source of my pain and the foundation of all of my negative behaviors. Inner-child work helped me recognize how my abusive childhood was still affecting my behavior some thirty years later. Some people believe that it isn't necessary to "dig up" old wounds to be transformed, but in my case, it was the one thing that really helped me heal my heart. Uncovering the hidden hurts released me from their unconscious grip. Inner-child work was the process that set my heart free. The amazing thing about inner-child work was that it helped me recognize the "why" of my behavior. Although I was always highly motivated and ambitious, this work taught me the reasons behind my motivation. All of the motivational seminars I attended prior to my participation simply fueled my deep feelings of inadequacy. I learned I was always motivated because I had this insatiable need to gain other people's approval. By recognizing this fact, I was able to learn to love myself regardless of any of my accomplishments. Once I let go of my need to impress other people, I freed myself to be as motivated as I wanted to be. But with my new understanding, I was authentically motivated. This is the truth that set me free.

Through the process of inner-child work, I reconnected with my emotions, and it has brought me joy and peace beyond description.

Another important piece of healing my heart was journaling. I began journaling as a result of my experience with a therapist. Journaling is an amazing process and one of the most effective ways of healing your heart. It allows you to access deep-rooted feelings and beliefs about yourself that may be the cause of the pain and suffering in your life. Learning to journal not only helped me discover who I am, it also uncovered the hidden writer inside of me that I did not know existed.

Expanding My Mind

Without question, my saving grace has been my love and passion for learning. From a very early age, I have always loved reading and learning new things. With all of today's technology, there is absolutely no reason for a person not to engage in expanding their mind. The Internet is an inexhaustible resource of information, which provides the perfect vehicle for expanding your mind and intellect. I personally love the Internet and technology because it gives me access to any information I need on any subject. With access to this information, I can always learn new things and expand my mind.

I also commit to reading a minimum of six new books a year. Although I probably average a lot more than this, I make sure that I read at least six. I believe that reading is for the mind what exercise is for the body. This is my exercise for my brain, and it keeps my intellect sharp, and my decision-making skills at their best.

Another great resource for expanding my mind is seminars. I must admit that I am a self-confessed seminar junkie. I love intellectually stimulating conversations and learning from some of the world's great minds. Seminars give me exposure to new ways of thinking and perceiving the world, and they challenge me to get out of my comfort zone and see things from a new and different perspective. What's wonderful about the Internet and technology is that I can attend seminars in the comfort of my own home on my computer without having to interact with anyone personally. But whenever I feel the need to engage face-to-face with like-minded people, I simply participate in a seminar or workshop that fulfills my need to interact and learn with others.

There is absolutely no excuse for people not to expand their minds and learn new things. The only thing that can prevent people from doing this is themselves.

Developing My Spiritual Connection

Although I will go into more detail in Chapter 9, I did want to briefly share some of the things I do to deepen my spiritual connection.

First and foremost, I had to come to my own truth about God. I had to become willing to admit that there was a power greater than myself in the universe. After I was able to accept this truth, I had to develop my own spiritual practices that insure that I deepen my relationship with this power. Here are three things that I do that help me deepen my spiritual connection.

Prayer

Prayer to me is simply having an ongoing dialog with my Creator. By communicating with my source, I develop a deep level of intimacy and connection to that which is greater than myself. This prayer takes many forms. It can be reading a spiritual message or listening to a spiritual messenger and then engaging in a conversation about what I heard, or it can mean having an attitude of gratitude for being alive. Prayer to me is simply concentrated thought. As long as I'm thinking about that which is greater than myself, I am actually engaged in prayer.

Meditation

One thing that I learned as a result of my transformation was the importance of meditation. Meditation is one of the greatest gifts that I have ever given myself. Meditation is my way of staying connected to my source, and it calms my spirit and eases my mind. It is only through the process of meditation that I was able to learn to quiet my mind so I could learn to listen to that still, small voice of wisdom within me. It is an extremely important aspect of my transformation, and it is something that I wholeheartedly recommend that you consider doing for yourself.

Contemplation

Contemplation is the process of thinking intently about God. To assist me in this process, I subscribe to several different spiritual resources that send me daily spiritual e-mails. As I read the e-mails and contemplate their messages, it deepens my awareness and understanding of God. By being willing to engage in this deep contemplation, I come to my own truth and understanding about God and it puts my heart at ease.

There you have them: prayer, meditation and contemplation, the three keys to deepening your spiritual connection.

TRANSFORMATION

These are some things that I do to keep my transformation permanently embedded in my heart, mind, and spirit. If any of these feel right to you, check them out and participate. I believe that if you truly set an intention to commit to your own transformation, you will be divinely guided to the perfect people and experiences to assist you in the process. Always remember the three steps to permanent transformation, make a commitment to these three steps and your life will be transformed for the better.

Step 1. Heal your heart.

Step 2. Expand your mind and intellect.

Step 3. Develop a spiritual connection with something greater than yourself.

Once you commit to permanent transformation, an amazing thing will happen. You will then become what I like to call an Authentic Male. An authentic male is a man who has taken the time to discover who he really is, and he never gets caught in any of the five illusions of manhood. As a result of discovering who he really is, he also learns to remove any of the five masks of masculinity he may have been wearing, and he is then able to be open, transparent, and vulnerable in any situation. The authentic male knows who he is and knows exactly what he wants from life and he is willing to do whatever it takes to live his dreams and create a fulfilling and meaningful existence.

Once you become an authentic male, then there are four cornerstones of authentic masculinity that you must embrace. These four cornerstones should be the foundation of your existence and the base from which you express your authentic self. Here are the four cornerstones of an authentic male.

Faith

The first cornerstone is faith. This means that a man develops an intimate relationship with the divine. He must choose the path that nurtures his soul and recognize that there is a power greater than himself that he has direct access to. He commits to nurturing his relationship with the divine and uses spiritual principles in all of his interactions in life and with others.

Accountability

The second cornerstone is accountability, which means that a man holds himself accountable for all of his actions and never places unjust blame on anyone else. He recognizes that his word is his bond, and that his word is sacred and can be counted on no matter what.

Integrity

The third cornerstone is Integrity. This means a man does what's right even when he doesn't have to. It means living from a moral and spiritual code that aligns with his core values and principles. It means trusting his still, small voice within and letting it guide him through life. As a man of integrity, he knows what is expected of him, and his actions are always congruent with the principles of an authentic male.

Responsibility

The fourth cornerstone is responsibility. This means that a man takes complete responsibility for his emotional, intellectual, physical and spiritual well-being. He takes the time to heal his heart and gains a deep understanding of who he is and why he is here. He recognizes that he must take complete responsibility for his life and success, and he knows that no one and nothing can stop him from living his dreams.

Think of the four cornerstones as the acronym FAIR:

Faith **A**ccountability **I**ntegrity **R**esponsibility

When a man learns to be fair with life, I can assure you that life returns the favor. My hope is that you embrace this new way of being a man and create your best life right now. If you become an authentic male I can assure you that life takes on a magical quality filled with excitement and adventure. But it's all up to you. Will you choose to become an authentic male?

If you need assistance in locating articles, seminars, or books to assist you in your transformation, be sure and check out our website at www.anewconversationwithmen.com.

I wish you joy, happiness and inner peace along your journey. Good luck!

"If we are completely honest with ourselves, the most beautiful gift we are given in this lifetime is a loving and caring spouse. (If we are fortunate enough to find the right one.) Her love, nurturing, and support are the glue that holds our lives together and is an integral part of our happiness and fulfillment. It is our responsibility as men to never neglect, abuse, or demean our women in any way, and we should never take our women for granted.
We must commit to opening our hearts and sharing ourselves with our women in a way that brings us closer together and creates a bond that lasts forever."

— Michael Taylor

Chapter Six

What's Love Got to Do with It?

When I was a young boy, I remember dreaming of being married and having kids and living happily ever after. In my dream, everything was perfect. I had a beautiful wife, some wonderful children, lots of money in the bank, and tons of freedom to do anything I wanted to do whenever I wanted to do them.

I believe the reason I had those dreams was that in reality, my life was the complete opposite. I was the product of a single parent home, living in poverty, with absolutely no evidence that my dream of the perfect family could ever come true. I had never been exposed to the type of wealth, unconditional love and nurturing seen on television, yet there was a longing in my soul to experience that type of family setting showcased in the soap operas and sitcoms. I believe that my dreams were simply a way for me to cope with all of the dysfunction that surrounded me.

As I look back, I realize that it was this particular dream that was the driving force to my success. I wanted more than anything to have the "perfect family" and to live happily ever after.

In the pursuit of my dream, I have come to the conclusion that the most important thing in a man's life is his relationships. Relationships are the glue that holds our lives together, and without them, life really has no real meaning or significance. Without our romantic, parental, professional, and spiritual relationships, our lives fall apart and become broken and disconnected. As a result, we experience unimaginable pain and suffering and then turn to addictive behaviors to try to cope with our discomfort and our loss.

Without rewarding and fulfilling relationships, we are like sailboats at sea without sails, floating aimlessly through life with no sense of purpose or direction. Without the love and support of the people we care about, it is impossible to navigate a course through life that will bring us to the destination that our souls long for. The harbor we long for is the harbor of unconditional love and acceptance. This is the safe haven of our souls that we must eventually dock into. Until we do, something will always be missing in our hearts.

So, if relationships are so important, why are they so difficult to create? Why do men struggle so much with creating and maintaining relationships? Why does this country have a divorce rate of approximately 50%?

Although there are no easy answers to these questions, I believe that *A New Conversation with Men* opens the door to a new dialog that can help us find some answers. My job is to not only provide some answers, but more importantly, raise the questions so that you can come to your own conclusions. It is ultimately up to you to listen to that still, small voice within you to answer your own questions.

This chapter is about creating a new conversation about relationships for men. It is our opportunity to create a new paradigm of behavior in our relationships that will ultimately assist us in creating rewarding and fulfilling experiences in our romantic and personal relationships.

A NEW CONVERSATION WITH MEN

I would like to begin by sharing a joke with you. This joke is incredibly funny, but at the same time, it is tragically sad. As you read the joke, check inside yourself for the thoughts and feelings you experience as you read it. See if you relate, and if so, ask yourself if you are willing to change your perceptions about relationships. Here's the joke:

A man and his ever-nagging wife went on vacation to Jerusalem. While they were there, the wife passed away. The undertaker told the husband, "You can have her shipped home for $5000, or you can bury her here, in the Holy Land, for $150." The man thought about it and told him he would have her shipped home.

The undertaker asked, "Why would you spend $5000 to ship your wife home when it would be wonderful to be buried here, and you would only spend $150?"

The man replied, "Long ago a man died here, was buried here, and three days later, he rose from the dead. I just can't take that chance."

So what did you think? Are you still laughing? The first time I read this joke, I laughed for five minutes. After that time, I began to think about the content and the context in which it was written and I realized it was sadder than it was funny. It is sad because there are far too many men who actually feel that way about their wives.

Instead of focusing on the problems, let's now turn our attention to some concrete solutions to help us improve our relationships. Despite the current assumptions about men and relationships, I actually remain optimistic that men are now open and willing to have a new conversation about relationships. In this new conversation, men will learn to create loving, caring, nurturing and fulfilling relationships that truly nurture their spirits. In doing so, we will begin to see a steady decline in high divorce rates, domestic violence, addictions, and violent crimes.

The reason I remain optimistic is because I believe that men are going through an evolutionary cycle. This evolutionary cycle is not based on Darwin's theory of evolution but rather my own theory of how men are evolving. My theories are based on my own research and are actually my own personal opinions and beliefs about men. I am not going to provide you with scientific statistics (I really dislike statistics) or scientifically substantiated proof. I am simply going to share my perceptions of the status of men in society and where I believe men are headed in regard to relationships.

It is my opinion and belief that there are five stages of evolution that males have gone through. As I share these five stages, simply ask yourself if they make sense to you. Try to take a global view because this evolutionary process is global. Men around the globe have gone through and continue to go through this process. It does not matter what country you're from or what part of the world you were born into. The five stages of evolution for males are:

The Caveman Male The Warrior Male The Religious Male The Scientific Male The Authentic Male

The Caveman Male

This is where it all began. The caveman male had three basic responsibilities. First, he was responsible for securing shelter. His job was to find a cave that kept him out of the elements and provided protection from those carnivorous dinosaurs that were trying to have him for dinner. Second, he was responsible for finding a mate to insure the continuation of the species. Third, he was responsible for feeding and protecting his family. It was his job to literally bring home the bacon (or whatever prehistoric equivalent there was to a pig) and at the same time make sure he did not become a meal himself. His primary objective was simply survival.

With the exception of inclement weather and the occasional run-in with saber-tooth tigers, the caveman male had a pretty good life. He did everything on instinct and relied solely on his intuition and gut feelings. That is how he survived and thrived. These instincts and gut feelings led him to amazing discoveries, which propelled him to evolve into the warrior male.

The Warrior Male

The warrior male had the same responsibilities as the caveman male, but the warrior male had developed language. Language allowed the warrior male to expand on the discoveries of the caveman male and develop new tools and new weapons that the caveman male did not have access to. With the addition of language, the warrior male begins communicating in new and different ways with his surroundings. This new form of communication allowed him to expand his awareness and ultimately led him to conclude that he was different from anyone who did not look like him or behave like him. With this way of viewing the world, his primary objective became conquering anyone who he perceived to be different. This led to war and separation amongst men. After several hundreds of years, the warrior male had to continue to evolve to ensure the continuation of the species and therefore the religious male was formed.

The Religious Male

As a way of removing some of the violent and inhumane acts against men, the religious male was born. This was the result of the emergence of highly evolved human beings that taught new ways of being men in society. These spiritual masters demonstrated that it was possible to live in peace and harmony with each other, and they provided spiritual principles that taught men how to live together. Unfortunately, their teachings were sometimes misinterpreted and abused, and they became the foundation for more wars and killings in the name of spiritual teachers. Eventually, men began to reject the teachings of the spiritual masters and started to rely strictly on science and intellectual understanding to try to solve people's problems. This led to new technological breakthroughs which created the next step in male evolution, which was the scientific male.

The Scientific Male

The scientific male relies solely on his intellect and science to solve problems. He is constantly looking outside of himself for answers and relies on technology to help fix whatever ails him. He realizes that he has access to things like television and the Internet, and he places most of his faith in material things. He exhibits qualities of the caveman male, the warrior male, and the religious male, but his primary focus is on "external" things. As a result, he has experienced emptiness and disconnection which is now propelling him towards new ways of being a man. He is tired of looking for external validation and is seeking something real, something that he can invest his soul into, something with meaning and fulfillment. The only way he can experience this is to evolve into the authentic male.

The Authentic Male

The authentic male is the culmination of all aspects of being male. It is taking the best of all aspects and combining them into a highly aware, intuitive man who is completely conscious and awake to who he is as a man. The authentic male knows who he is, and he is able to be authentic and transparent in all of his interactions with others. He recognizes that there is a part of him that is like the caveman male that must be responsible for providing shelter and food for himself and his family. He knows that he has a warrior spirit that encourages him to challenge his own fears and move through them without hesitation. He embraces his religious male by developing a spiritual connection that nurtures his soul, and he supports his scientific male by expanding his intellect and making use of current technology.

But ultimately, he knows that he needs absolutely nothing outside of himself to be validated. He is the authentic male and he knows without question that he is lovable and acceptable just the way he is without any external thing. He recognizes and accepts the fact that he is not perfect, and simultaneously he knows that in actuality, he is perfect as a result of his imperfections. He is able to live and love deeply, and he is committed to having and maintaining relationships that nurture his mind, body, and spirit. He refuses to accept mediocrity in any form, and he strives to become the best man that he can be. His relationships are his highest priority, and therefore, he measures his success by the depth of his relationships.

For this reason, I am so optimistic about men and the future. I strongly believe that men are evolving into the authentic male and in doing so, we will create the new paradigm of masculinity that I speak about. It is this shift in awareness that will propel men into a new conversation that will ultimately assist in healing the world.

Since this chapter is about creating great relationships, let's answer some very basic questions that most men have in regard to creating and maintaining healthy fulfilling relationships.

Why are relationships so difficult?

My honest opinion is that relationships are difficult only when men are trapped in one of the five illusions or are wearing one of the five masks of masculinity. When a man takes the time to become an authentic male, relationships then become rewarding and fulfilling experiences that can truly nurture a man's soul. Unfortunately, most men are hesitant about taking the time to get to know who they really are. This unwillingness to address our emotional and psychological issues is what keeps men from creating relationships that really work, and that is why they can be so difficult.

Is it really possible for a man to be happy and fulfilled in a monogamous relationship?

Absolutely, unequivocally yes! Despite what you may believe or have seen throughout our media, it is definitely possible for a man to have a rewarding, fulfilling monogamous relationship. In a non-scientific poll, I asked the question: Can men create monogamous relationships? The survey revealed that 87% of men believe that men can be monogamous. My belief is that most men actually would rather be monogamous, but most of us aren't willing to invest in gaining the emotional tools to make a monogamous relationship rewarding and fulfilling. In order to do this, we have to incorporate things like sensitivity, vulnerability, and intimacy into our vocabulary and into our actions, and that is absolutely terrifying to some men. But without them, a happy and fulfilling relationship isn't possible.

If a man is committed to becoming an authentic male, I can assure you that he will seek out and create a loving, caring and connected relationship.

Why is it so difficult for a man to be emotionally available in relationships?

As mentioned throughout this book, men have been conditioned not to feel. From a very young age, we are taught that it's bad to be emotional, it's weak to be sensitive, and only women have access to intuition. This denial of our very basic emotions keeps us from being able to connect on an emotional and spiritual level. It does not mean we are incapable of being emotionally available, it means most of us aren't willing to learn how. Most of us do not have the emotional tools needed to be available in this way, but the fact of the matter is we do have the capacity to learn. This is our greatest challenge, in my opinion. Our feelings are the language of our souls, and it is absolutely mandatory that we learn to feel, connect, and express our feelings openly and honestly. This is not a sign of weakness but a sign of strength. It is a surefire way to become an authentic male.

I believe the reason most men reject their emotions is that we have been conditioned to believe that getting in touch with our emotions means getting in touch with our "feminine" side. As soon as we stop labeling emotions as feminine, I believe more men will engage in this conversation because being labeled as feminine in any form is a direct attack on the sensitive male ego. Emotions are neither feminine nor masculine. Women do not hold a monopoly on emotions. They have simply been conditioned to be comfortable expressing their emotions. It is socially and culturally accepted. Emotions are simply energy in motion, and it is important that a person simply learns to identify this energy that is moving through them. When we can accept this fundamental fact that it isn't feminine to be in touch with your emotions, men will then be able to connect with their emotions and therefore become emotionally available in relationships.

Why do most people have less sex after they get married?

It is probably the most pleasurable experience that human beings have. It excites us, delights us, and drives us absolutely insane. We write songs about it, make movies about it, tell lies about it, and even daydream about it. By some accounts, men think about it every 52 seconds. The experience of sex is incredible, and nothing gives us more pleasure and at the same time causes us more pain.

If you watch our media, you should notice that we are constantly bombarded with images of sex and nudity. As the saying goes, "Sex sells," and the marketers and advertisers make sure that they take every opportunity to take advantage of this adage. Companies use sex to sell everything from golf clubs to chicken wings, and each year, the advertising seems to get more and more provocative.

With this over-proliferation of sexual images, one might conclude that everyone is engaged in sex 24 hours a day, seven days a week. Not only do we assume everyone is doing it, we also assume that they are actually enjoying doing it! But if sex is so wonderful and pleasurable, why are so many people so unhappy with their sex lives? Why is it that married couples tend to have less sex as time goes by?

Why do people have affairs for sex when they should have access to all the sex they want if they have a committed relationship? Why do people have so much difficulty being honest about how they really feel about sex and have to lie and make up excuses for their sexual behaviors and appetites? Although there are numerous answers to these questions, I have come to the conclusion that there is one answer that really covers the gamut of most of these questions.

This one answer is so simple yet so complex that very few people will grasp its implication. The answer is so profoundly simple that you probably will not believe it. If you have ever wondered why men obsess over sex yet remained unfilled, I have the answer. If you have asked why people have affairs, this will answer that question. If you get caught up in power struggles over sex, this answer will shed light on the reason. And if you have ever wondered why it is so difficult to maintain a fulfilling sex life, I have the key.

Would you like the key that will unlock the door to great sex? Are you willing to contemplate this answer so that you can create and maintain a wonderful, fulfilling sexual relationship with your partner?

WHAT'S LOVE GOT TO DO WITH IT?

Here it is, the million-dollar answer you have been waiting for. People are unhappy with their sex lives because our society has conditioned us to believe that sex is purely a physical experience, when in truth, it should be an emotional and a spiritual experience! Without the emotional and spiritual aspect of sex, people will always feel as if something is missing. It does not matter if you cause your mate to have powerful orgasms that send shivers up and down her spine. It does not matter if you have two-hour erections (dream on) that would make you an instant star in a pornographic movie. If your emotions are not involved, sex will always be empty and unfulfilling. You may experience temporary pleasure, but ultimately, if you will really examine your feelings, you will feel in your heart that something just isn't right. This is why so many men are uncomfortable with cuddling after sex. If you are emotionally and spiritually connected with your mate, then cuddling is a continuation of the sexual experience. Opening your heart and mind to the experience will always bring you closer to your mate. But most of us are very uncomfortable with this type of openness and vulnerability.

The reason so many of us are unhappy is that we seek physical pleasure without emotional attachment, and that is a recipe for addiction. In order to truly experience lovemaking and intimacy, we must be able to feel the energy of love moving through us as we connect with our mate. We must learn to open our hearts and expose our true selves so that our partners can emotionally and spiritually unite with us. This may sound like something out of a romance novel, but it is an attainable experience if you focus on the emotional aspect of your sexual encounters. Most of us are so committed to "getting laid" and simply "getting some" that we miss out on the most important aspect of sex, which is sharing yourself with your mate in the emotional and spiritual act of lovemaking. The time has come for all men to learn to make love to their mates and not just have sex with them.

Although most men will probably not admit this, we can be terrified of this level of intimacy because in the back of our minds, we may be afraid to surrender our hearts to the people we love. Some of us keep up emotional blocks because we are too afraid to have that type of trust and connection.

It sometimes seems easier to simply sleep around with multiple women to prove our manhood, but the truth is, we pay a heavy price for this detached way of behaving. A real man will take the risk and open his heart because in the end, he recognizes that true love is about openness and surrender. He takes the risks to love, and he is rewarded with love and connection.

Did you know that you could make love to your mate and never physically touch her? If this sounds impossible, then you are trapped in the illusion of physical sex. True love is a function of the heart and mind and has absolutely nothing to do with your penis. If you really want to make love, leave your penis in your pants and learn to take out your heart and share it with your mate.

To sum it up, many people stop having sex because when you first meet someone, sex is more about physical pleasure than emotional intimacy. As a relationship deepens, it must have the emotional connection and intimacy in order to flourish. Without it, the relationship will always dissolve. As the lack of emotional connection becomes evident, people then feel a void and an emptiness inside. When this emptiness is experienced, sex has no place in the relationship.

Why do some men cheat?

First of all, I'll begin by saying that men aren't the only ones who engage in infidelity. Unfortunately, women are beginning to catch up with men in this category based on some reports.

But to answer the question, it is my fervent belief that affairs are never really about sex. People cheat to try to fill an unfulfilled emotional need. While it may appear that the man is searching for sex, I do not believe that is the case. Because some men are disconnected from their feelings, they begin to process everything through their intellect. In their minds, they rationalize their feelings and then justify their actions by thinking they are doing the right thing. This thinking is just a defense mechanism that some men use to keep them from feeling their emotions. It's been said that all addictive behaviors are the result of unresolved emotional conflict. If a man becomes courageous enough to resolve his emotional conflict, then his addictive behaviors will disappear.

Most people believe that men have some sort of animal instinct that makes them crave sex, but I totally disagree with that notion. Men are not animals, and they have the ability to discern right from wrong. Every man is completely responsible for his actions whether he will admit that or not. Another reason I believe some men cheat is that they are trapped in the illusion that to be a man, he must achieve sexual conquest. This underlying illusion has caused lots of heartache in many men's lives. In addition, if he is wearing the Mr. Sex Man mask, then he will always act out in sexual ways and rationalize his actions by saying that he's just a man.

There are really no secrets to creating great relationships. The first thing we must do is learn to create a great relationship with ourselves.

This means taking the time to understand who we really are and becoming authentic males. Once we do this, I can assure you that relationships become rewarding and fulfilling.

Take some time and really think about this. I hope that this becomes fuel for contemplation, which challenges you to look within yourself and find your own answers. I can assure you that great relationships are possible if you will heed the advice of going within so you do not have to go without.

Now, I would like to share five ways to know if you really love your mate. These five simple things can be used to gauge just how connected you are to your significant other. Read over them and see if you relate.

1. If you truly love your mate, you can be honest with her about how you really feel. This means that you can tell her when you are angry or you can tell her when you are sad or afraid. If you really do not like those new shoes she bought, you can tactfully be honest and say you do not like them. You can express yourself openly and honestly when things aren't going well in your life. You are able to share the good and the bad with her. In other words, you can truly communicate with each other. This means that you are able to speak from your heart, not your head, which means that you are emotionally available.

2. If you truly love your mate, whenever something significant occurs in your life, she is the first person that you want to tell. Your spouse should be the most important person in your life. Therefore, she should be the first person that comes to mind whenever you experience triumph or tragedy. She should be

the person you can count on no matter what the situation. Is she the first person that comes to mind when you are faced with tragedy or triumph?

3. If you truly love your mate, even when she gets on your last nerve and you're mad as hell, you still know that this is the woman that you want to spend the rest of your life with. You never think about leaving, and you know that you can work through anything. As the saying goes, "This too shall pass," and you recognize this divine truth. You recognize the difference between who she is and what she does, and you can be angry temporarily at what she does, but you are never angry with who she really is. You understand that relationships are perfect in their imperfection, and you accept her imperfections as well as your own.

4. If you truly love your mate, then you commit to spending quality time with her. This does not mean that you have to take her out or spend any money on her. It simply means that you give her your undivided attention and share in her interests sometimes. It's amazing how the most important relationship in our lives is often neglected, and then we wonder why we end up in divorce court. If you really love your mate, why wouldn't you want to be with her? Spend some time with your mate, and have some fun together. My wife and I are both off on Fridays. This is her day, and I will usually go wherever she wants to go. I may not necessarily like where we are going, but I make it a point to make the most of it if she really enjoys it. Most of us get so caught up with jobs and families and mortgages and stress that we neglect our mates and ourselves. Slow down a

little, and make some time for you and your mate. Everyone in your life will benefit when you do.

5. If you really and truly love your mate you are never tempted to stray even if the woman who may be tempting you looks better and is finer than she is. There will always be someone better looking than your mate. If you truly love someone, it is about more than their physical beauty; it should also be about their inner beauty, and when you connect with that, your love will truly flourish. True love is more than just a feeling. It is a commitment and an action that says that you have dedicated your life to this person and this person only. Your commitment is to be faithful. Isn't that the reason you married her in the first place? You must realize that a temporary attraction is okay as long as you do not allow yourself to act on that momentary attraction. If we really love our mates, then there is no way we could ever cheat on them because we would be able to feel the hurt and devastation that betrayal causes, and we would never want our wives to feel that terrible pain. Some men rationalize, (which means they tell rational lies to themselves) that as long as they provide for their families, it's okay to be unfaithful. The truth is that they may love their wives but they are definitely not in love with them. That is the distinction that most men really struggle with. The time has come for us to learn how to be in love with our mates, and that can only be accomplished when we learn to love ourselves first. This takes emotional openness and honesty, but it is the key to creating a relationship that lasts.

With this country's current divorce rate hovering around 50%, I think it is extremely important that we as men make a concerted effort to create and maintain great relationships. If you happen to be single and are considering marriage, I would like to share my top five reasons why a person should not get married, as well as the top five reasons that they should. Take some time and ponder these and see if any apply to your current situation.

Top Five Reasons a Person Should Not Be Getting Married

1. Never get married because you think you are supposed to. Duty and obligation are not a good foundation to build a marriage on. Do not get caught on the societal roller coaster and think that being married automatically makes you happier. If your parents are nagging you, or your friends are pressuring you, don't pay attention to them. Learn to listen to your own heart, and trust it to guide you in making the right decision for yourself. The key is to make sure that you have healed your heart so that you can connect to what it may be telling you.

2. Never get married because of GSSS (Great Steady Safe Sex). People who get married only because of great sex are in for a very rude awakening. Great sex is usually based on physical pleasure, and that is always temporary. In order to create a great marriage, you must have emotional openness and intimacy. If you create a relationship with these two values, there is no way that you will not have great sex.

3. Never get married because you are lonely and believe you need someone else to complete you. If you do not feel complete with yourself, you will never feel complete with someone else. Have you ever heard the saying that you should never go shopping when you are hungry? There is a reason why you should listen to this; when you are hungry, your eyes become bigger than your stomach, and you'll end up eating the first thing that you get to. Your intention is to fulfill the hunger, and a lot of times you aren't thinking rationally when you start eating that half gallon of Bluebell ice cream. Marriage is the same way; if you are lonely, you will not be thinking rationally, and your intention will be to fulfill the loneliness instead of creating a wonderful relationship. So make sure that you spend some time to fall in love with yourself before you begin looking for someone to love.

4. Never get married for financial security in and of itself. There is absolutely nothing wrong with marrying someone with money, but if you are specifically looking for someone to take care of you financially, you will end up becoming a slave to your financial master. If you take a look at some couples that have lots of money yet they argue and fight over every little financial detail and decision, that is not a marriage filled with trust, openness, and joy; instead, that is a marriage filled with resentment, anger, and unhappiness. Do you really want to experience that?

5. Do not get married just for the kids or because you are pregnant. Kids intuitively know when parents aren't happy.

If you are getting married because you feel obligated to your children, it will come back to haunt you later. If you are marrying out of obligation and fear, then your marriage will end up being filled with both. Eventually, you will resent your spouse and yourself as well, and you will definitely not be happy.

Top Five Reasons to Get Married

1. If you have taken the time to truly understand who you are and feel whole and complete within yourself, marriage can be a wonderful thing. Having someone that appreciates, respects, adores, and loves you for who you are is one of life's greatest gifts. I believe that we human beings are wired to find compatible people to share life with. It's actually encoded in our DNA to love and to be loved. Although you do not have to be married to experience love, my belief is that the commitment of marriage can and should deepen your level of love and intimacy.

2. It's been statistically proven that married people are happier, healthier, and live longer than single people, not to mention the reduced amount of stress that comes from having a happy marriage. If given the choice between a joyful marriage or a wild-and-free single life, I'd choose the joyful marriage every time.

3. GSSS! Great Steady Safe Sex. As I mentioned earlier, if two people are committed to communicating openly and honestly about their emotional and physical needs, there

is absolutely no way that they will not experience great sex. The problem is that we put so much emphasis on the physical aspect of sex that we negate the emotional and spiritual aspects of making love. One of the greatest challenges men have is to learn to make love to their mates instead of just having sex with them. Making love includes being emotionally and spiritually in tune with your partner in addition to being open and honest about your own sexual needs. When we learn to create an open, honest dialog about sex in our marriage, then we can create a passionate and fulfilling sex life.

4. There are definitely financial advantages to being married. Although I believe that you should marry for love and commitment, it is not contradictory to mention the financial benefits of being married. When two people have the same financial goals and objectives, it is easier to achieve them when they are working together. Two bank accounts grow faster than one. Just make sure that the love, joy, and intimacy come first, and then enjoy the financial rewards as an end result.

5. Life is simply more fun when you have someone to share it with. Again, I state that you do not have to be married to have fun with someone, but I believe that marriage can definitely enhance the experience if the two people are committed to the same thing. Although I enjoy my own personal time and have no problem doing things alone, I really enjoy sharing my life with my wife. Knowing that I have a partner to share my life

with is emotionally comforting to me. I prefer being married instead of single for this very reason.

These are my five reasons to be married. What do you think? Do you agree or disagree with what I have written? As usual, I am simply providing you with fuel for contemplation. You get to choose what to do with the fuel. You can use it to ignite passion in your relationship, or use it to propel you far away from love and commitment back to the old ways of being a man in which you feel isolated and disconnected. What will you choose?

After reading this chapter, I hope that you have concluded that relationships do not have to be war zones in which each person is either attacking or afraid of being attacked. You should not have to relate to your wife as "The old ball and chain," and you shouldn't feel as if you have been given a prison sentence because you are married. Marriage and relationships really can be wonderful experiences. They can be filled with authentic love and appreciation, and they can nurture you in ways that nothing else can. So, when it's all said and done and you're lying on your death bed, I can assure you that knowing that you have given and received love is going to be much more important than all the "stuff" you accumulated throughout your life. In the end, you will be able to reflect back on your life with no regrets and say to yourself, "Well done."

In this new conversation, my hope is that men begin to recognize just how important our relationships really are. Our country is built on strong family units, and it is imperative that we do all that we can to lower the divorce rates and provide our children with stable, loving families. This is the key to keeping this country strong, and we must all work together. To accomplish this, I believe we must have a new conversation about relationships and in doing so, we lay the foundation for the eradication of the majority of the social ills affecting our country. Together, we can make it happen.

Just remember that it starts with the man in the mirror.

"Your children are not your children.
They are the sons and daughters
of life's longing for itself.
They come through you but not from you,
And though they are with you, yet they
belong not to you."

— Khalil Gibran, from *The Prophet*

Chapter Seven

Fatherlessness

It is my fervent belief that one of the greatest challenges we have in our society is fatherlessness. To give you an idea of how negatively this issue affects our country, consider these statistics. Did you know that some studies have shown that:

85% of all children that exhibit behavioral disorders come from fatherless homes?

90% of all homeless and runaway children are from fatherless homes? 71% of all high school dropouts come from fatherless homes?

75% of all adolescent patients in chemical abuse centers come from fatherless homes?

63% of youth suicides are from fatherless homes?

80% of rapists motivated by displaced anger come from fatherless homes?

70% of juveniles in state-operated institutions come from fatherless homes?

85% of all youths sitting in prisons grew up in a fatherless home?

Now, some of you reading this may have accepted the media-generated illusion that fatherlessness is a black/minority problem. You may also have accepted the illusion that it is an inner-city economic problem. The fact of the matter is that this problem transcends race, economics, social status, and religious background. It is a problem that affects all aspects of our society, and it is going to take all aspects of our society to resolve it.

In order for us to resolve these issues, I believe it is absolutely imperative that we begin a new conversation with men. In this new conversation, we will recognize that we will never create solutions to these problems with new legislation or public policy. Politicians cannot solve these issues because no law can be passed nor any fine be assessed to make a man become a good father. Fatherlessness is not a political problem; therefore, we cannot rely on political means to resolve it.

Another thing we must recognize is that being a good father is not genetic. There is no such thing as a good-father gene that is passed on from family to family from generation to generation. Being a great father is a learned behavior, and therefore, every man can learn to become a great father if he chooses. Becoming a great father is a choice. It is up to each individual man to consciously choose to become a good father, and then, he must be willing to educate himself so that he has the emotional and intellectual tools to parent his child and be a good role model.

So what about you? Are you willing to engage in this new conversation? Are you willing to make the choice to become the very best father you could possibly be? Are you committed to doing your part, first by taking care of your own children, and secondly by sharing this information with others to assist them in becoming better fathers? Once again, I welcome you to *A New Conversation with Men*!

Before I share my solutions for fatherlessness, I believe it is important to recognize that there are lots of men who are currently doing a great job as fathers. As a matter of fact, I believe most men are doing good jobs, but our commitment must be to do great jobs. When it comes to being fathers to our children, we must not settle for mediocrity; we must commit to excellence. So I'd like to begin by acknowledging all fathers who are leading by example and serving as great role models for their children. I thank you, and I know your children and family thank you as well.

Now, I would like to share my ten steps to removing fatherlessness from our society. These ten steps are the actual steps I have used in my own life to be a great father, and I share them because I know they work. I learned these steps as a result of the past fifteen years of research and I believe they can make a difference if you will apply the lessons to your life.

Step 1.
Men must recognize how our cultures and society have conditioned us not to be good fathers.

Throughout this book, I have talked about the impact and effects that the media and our cultures have on our belief systems. Some people may interpret this as my saying that the media is responsible for our behavior. This is incorrect. As I talk about societal conditioning, in no way am I blaming society for a man's behavior. Every man is 100%

responsible for his own actions and behavior. But I think it is extremely important to recognize that a lot of our behaviors are preconditioned responses that we engage in "unconsciously." It isn't until we recognize this fact that we can become conscious and then begin to make conscious changes to them. In other words, we must wake up so that we will make choices based on our current understandings and not past previous preconditioned reflexes.

Let me clarify what I mean by our society and cultures conditioning us not to be great fathers. Have you ever noticed that a lot of men say how much they love their children (which most men do) yet spend very little time with them? Some men work 50 or 60 hours a week to provide for their families, yet they have no real relationship with their children. They cannot simply sit down and speak lovingly with their children because they are too exhausted, too stressed, or downright frustrated with their jobs. The rationalization is that men must work hard to bring home the bacon and provide for their families, and yet, when they are at home, they do not necessarily know how to interact with their children. Since most men are disciplinarians, their duties are relegated to discipline and punishment instead of nurturing and encouragement, and therefore, the relationships with their children are often disconnected and discipline-oriented. The children see the father as the bad guy who is always doing the punishing and the mother as the good guy who is always loving and supportive.

The irony here is that we say that our children are really important to us, and we convince ourselves that we must work hard to provide for them to keep them happy. We think that by working hard and making more money, everyone will be happy. But it never works because we are unhappy that we have to work so much, and our kids are unhappy because they never see us or spend quality time with us. The last thing our children really need is for us to be stressed-out, unhappy workaholics who can't connect emotionally with them. But that is exactly what we become: stressed-out workaholics who believe we're making our children happy. How crazy is that? If we truly loved our children, wouldn't we make them our priority and make sure that we can spend quality time with them and not be stressed out and exhausted?

In order to compensate for our lack of emotional contributions to our children, we then fall into the trap of materialism and try to buy our children's love. By buying them all the latest toys and gadgets, we convince ourselves that we're really good fathers, and it temporarily removes the feelings of guilt and sadness we feel because we aren't spending quality time with them. If we would simply be honest with ourselves and admit that we actually want the same thing that our children want, which is to be loved unconditionally and to feel connected to our children, it would remove a lot of pain and suffering from our lives, but unfortunately, most of us are too "unconscious" to even admit this. So we do the best we can by buying more stuff, which unfortunately is a temporary fix that only leads to more unhappiness.

During this time, we've completely forgotten about the emotional needs of our spouse. Now she's complaining that we don't spend enough time with her, and she's feeling alone and separated. She tries to communicate to us that we're working too much but this only makes us angry because in our minds, we're working our tails off trying to provide for our families and now it feels like we're being attacked for trying to be a good husband.

Now we're really stressed. So what do we do now? We turn to the societal quick-fix stress relievers; alcohol or drugs! These two substances are the temporary fixes we use to try to cope with all of the unhappiness in our lives. We rationalize our behaviors by saying that we need a drink to take the edge off or to relax. We tell ourselves that this is the only way we can cope. We then continue to go to happy hour to try to alleviate the emotional pain and suffering in our hearts, and all of a sudden, we meet someone new we can talk to about all of the stress and challenges in our lives.

We are then trapped on the societal merry-go-round. This means that we're working extra hard to make money to keep everybody happy. Then we buy "stuff" because we feel guilty because we think nobody's happy. Now nobody is happy because we're working too much, and we're definitely unhappy because we're spending too much money, working too many hours, and everyone is complaining. In order to cope with the unhappiness, we turn to drugs and alcohol, but then, we get addicted and begin spiraling out of control. Now, this new "friend" has entered the picture, which really makes things complicated because she is now demanding more of our time and energy, which we definitely do not have. As a result of our inability to perform at work (in addition to our alcohol and drug addiction), we get fired. Now we're really unhappy because we aren't making any money at all, our wife wants to leave, our children are miserable, our self-esteem is shot, and we don't have a clue as to what happened. All we are left with are questions. What the hell happened? And how in the world did I get into this mess?

Can you relate? Does any of this sound familiar? This is the reason men must recognize how our cultures and society have conditioned us not to be good fathers. When we are unconscious of how societal conditioning affects us, we have no power over it. By becoming conscious, we can change our behaviors. The only way out is to become conscious and embrace a new conversation with yourself. In this new conversation, you will recognize the merry-go-round and be able to not get on it in the first place. But you must be willing to embrace some new ways of thinking and behaving as a man, and that is the purpose of this book.

Step 2.
We must be willing to examine our relationship with our own father.

Whether you are aware of it or not, your relationship with your father has a direct bearing on the relationship you will have with your own children. This is extremely important to know because it really does have a major impact on your ability to be a great father. If your father was loving, caring, supportive, and involved in your life, then there is a very good chance that you will interact with your children in the very same way. But if your father was violent, non-emotional, distant, and demanding, then it stands to reason that you will possibly end up being the same way with your children.

But no matter what type of father you may have had, you do not have to treat your children the way you were treated if you don't want to. You have the ability to break the cycle of violence and disconnection by learning new ways of being and interacting with your children. This is why this conversation is so important. The conversation provides you with insights and wisdom to help you make better choices in your life, which can assist you in becoming the best man you can be.

Take a moment and answer these questions:

Was your father around during the formative years of your life? (birth thru 16)

What is the fondest memory you have of your father? What is the worst memory?

Do you love or hate your father?

Do you feel yourself getting angry when you think about your father? Do you feel a sense of sadness when you think about your father?

Are you happy when you think of your father?

As you ask yourself these questions, try to be as honest as possible with yourself as you answer them. These questions intend to bring up any feelings you may have suppressed about your father so that you can identify them and decide if you would like to examine how these feelings may be affecting you today. This can be extremely difficult to do. But it is important that you allow yourself to feel whatever feelings come up for you, and then take action if you feel the need to. If you notice that you have very strong negative feelings come up, I can assure you that those repressed feelings are affecting you, possibly without your knowing about it. As these feelings arise, it may be a good idea to discuss them with a trusted friend or a therapist. By working with a therapist, they can help guide you through those emotions and give you some techniques to help you deal with the feelings.

Step 3. Healing our hearts.

Healing our hearts is actually the first step in becoming whole and authentic. There is nothing more important to being a great father than healing our hearts. If we will take the time to examine our childhood and heal any hurts from our past, then we lay the foundation for being great fathers. If there is unresolved emotional conflict in our hearts, then we can never expect to be the fathers I know we're capable of becoming.

If you had any negative emotions come up as a result of answering the above questions, then there is a distinct possibility that you need to engage in healing your heart. If you are always negative, judgmental, sarcastic, harbor hatred towards people of other races, or are the type of man who gets angry easily, there is a very good possibility that you need to heal your heart. Men who are constantly exhibiting negative, angry behavior are usually the ones with the most emotional wounds. It's important to recognize that their wounds are what causes their behavior, and even the angriest man has, at his core a heart of love and compassion. The challenge is for men to become courageous enough to begin examining their inner worlds so that they can resolve their emotional conflicts and become whole again. It is only through this healing process that men can learn to be loving, caring, nurturing, and supportive fathers.

Step 4.
Understand the importance of emotional connection.

Have you ever wondered how a man can abandon his children? Have you ever thought about the reasons some men will walk away from their child's life and never come back? Although there are no easy answers to this question, I can assure you that at the core of the answer is a man's inability to connect emotionally with his child. When a man does not have the emotional awareness and connection to his own heart, it is extremely difficult, if not impossible, for him to connect emotionally with his children. Therefore he is able to walk away from something that is really important to him because he really can't feel the pain of loss and disconnection from his child. When a man is emotionally connected to himself and his child, there is no way he could ever completely walk away from their lives. He may choose not to participate on a regular basis, but his heart would never allow him to completely disconnect from his children. The pain would be too great. This is the reason healing our hearts is so important. It allows us to feel connected. In feeling this connection, we allow ourselves to become great fathers who love, adore, and connect with our children, and we stay engaged in our child's life forever.

Step 5.
Commit to planning our families.

If we look at the number of unplanned pregnancies in our society, some of us conclude that it is the result of irresponsible teenagers from inner cities. The truth of the matter is that it's not just young women from the inner city who are getting pregnant. Women of all ages, races and socio-economic backgrounds are dealing with this challenge, and the time has come for us as men to step up to make sure that we minimize the number of unwanted pregnancies in our society. This means that we engage in open honest conversations with our women about sex and contraception from the beginning of our relationships. We can no longer simply engage in sex and hold the woman responsible for not getting pregnant. We must take a stand and be courageous enough to take charge and participate in preventing unwanted pregnancies. Too many men leave this burden on their women, but the time has come for us to step up as men and be responsible.

We must also wake men up from the illusion that sexual conquest is a gauge for manhood. This illusion is what drives too many men to father children that they have no intention of supporting or raising. As long as this illusion exists, we will continue to see a high number of unwanted pregnancies in our society. Men who are trapped in this illusion see creating babies as another gauge for masculinity. This is why it's so important to have this new conversation so that we can remove this illusion from our society and thereby minimize the number of unwanted pregnancies.

Although we relate unwanted pregnancies to single mothers, it's also important to recognize that married men must be responsible in planning for their children also. It's easy to get caught on the societal roller coaster and begin having babies right after we get married, but sometimes this isn't in our best interest. Men must be willing to engage in dialog with their wives and plan their pregnancies together. Not only should they discuss the emotional and psychological challenges of having children, they must also discuss the financial burdens that come with having children. Planning your children and working together as a team will remove a considerable amount of stress and anxiety from the relationship. The more we plan for having our children, the easier it will be to raise them.

Step 6.
Stay committed to your child forever.

No matter how you bring a child into this world, it is your responsibility to take care of it until it can take care of itself. I don't care if you think it was an accident or maybe you think the woman trapped you, if the child is yours, then you are responsible for it. (If you are afraid that you may end up in this situation, then all you have to do is follow the advice from the previous step and make sure that you do not end up with an unwanted pregnancy). No matter how that baby arrives, if it is yours, then you must commit to it forever. Even if you are not going to continue the relationship with the mother of the child, you must still take responsibility for it. Being committed to it means that you actively participate in its growth and nourishment. This does not mean that you will necessarily be there to feed it; it means that you will provide it with love, encouragement, and guidance to allow it to grow up emotionally, psychologically, and spiritually healthy.

Being committed means that you stay in touch and let your children know that they are loved and accepted. Your children should always know that you are their father even if you live in different cities or countries. With today's technologies, there is absolutely no excuse for you to not stay committed and connected to your child. If you remarry and have other children, it does not release you from the commitment to your first children. If you are man enough to continue having children, then you must be man enough to continue supporting all of them. You must be a man and find a way to always stay connected to your children no matter how many times you may remarry. Your children should always come first in your life. Stay committed, and be a great father.

Step 7.
Take responsibility for your child's emotional, physical and financial well-being.

Most of us were never taught just how important it is to talk to our children about major events that affect their lives. We assume that children are resilient and can easily bounce back from things like divorce, physical abuse, separation from their friends, or exposure to violence in their homes or on television. We assume that they are all right, and then we wonder why so many of our young people commit suicide and engage in violent behavior. It is important that we recognize that our children are emotionally fragile, and although they may not speak openly about their hurts and pains, their hearts ache, and their minds get clouded with all of the stresses of today's violent society. It is extremely important that we recognize when our children are dealing with emotional crises. The way to do this is to create an open line of communication with your children so that they will talk to you when they are hurting. This is so difficult to do because most of us really don't know how to create this open level of communication. If we have difficulty doing this, we must be willing to seek out resources to assist us. No matter what it takes, we must stay in tune with our children's emotional well-being and state of mind.

In addition to their emotional state, we must also stay aware of their physical state as well. This means that we help them watch their weight and help them make wise choices about the foods they eat and the things they put into their bodies. We talk to them about alcohol and drugs, and we try our best to keep them from ingesting any of the harmful and illegal things that can be so destructive to their lives.

Just as important as the emotional and physical is the financial well-being of our children. This means that we take financial responsibility for taking care of our children the best way that we can. Financial responsibility means that we teach our children to not be so caught up in material things, and we lead by example of not being so materialistic ourselves. It means that we become willing to give up lavish lifestyles and material things if that's what it takes to be financially responsible for our children. It also means that if we are divorced and not living with our children, then we adhere to any court-ordered child support and make sure that we are doing our part in raising our children. You shouldn't need a court order to want to take care of your child financially. It should be something that you do voluntarily irrespective of the circumstances. Of course, there may be times when you are not able to maintain your financial responsibilities, but you can always make up for it by staying in contact with your child and letting them know just how much they mean to you and letting them know how much you love them. Love may not pay the bills, but I can assure you that it pays for itself in the connection that you create with your child when you are truly committed and connected to them.

Step 8.
Be a trusted friend to your child.

This can be extremely difficult for men because we are taught that we are supposed to be the leaders and heads of households. Somehow, we have assumed that this prevents us from being friends with our children because we are afraid that this somehow makes us bad parents. Our fear is that if we become friends with our children, we will somehow lose the ability to "control" them, and therefore, they may begin to disrespect us. I completely disagree with this idea. My belief is that we should be both. We can be strong fathers that lead our families, and at the same time, we can develop friendships with our children that create open honest communication. This open, honest communication allows them to develop trust in us, which encourages them to speak openly about whatever may be going on in their lives. When we promote this idea that we are just fathers and that our word is law, we close the line of communication, and our children seek other people to speak openly with. By creating a friendly parental environment, I believe we create families that grow together and stay together.

Step 9.
Always keep your word to your child.

Although society has always said that a woman's nurturing has the greatest impact on a child's behavior, I believe that a man's interactions with a child are just as important or maybe even more important than a woman's when it comes to a child's self-esteem. Although I have no scientific evidence of this, I still hold firmly to the belief that men actually play a greater role in a child's psychological development than women.

With that as the basis for this step, I believe that nothing is more devastating to a child's self-esteem than a father who doesn't keep his word. Maybe the reason I feel this way is that I remember the disappointments from my own father, who would make promises he never kept. I still remember the pain and anguish that came from expecting him to do something and then not having him keep his word. I remember feeling angry and sad at the same time, in addition to a deep feeling of loneliness whenever he did not show up for a specific event that he promised he would attend. Amazingly, I used these negative memories to actually become a better man than my father. I remember how painful it felt as a child to be disappointed by my father, so I made a conscious effort to never disappoint my own children in the same way. I made it a point to always keep my promises. In a metaphysical kind of way, my pain and suffering actually made me a better man and a better father.

It's important to realize that keeping your word should be your top priority in raising your child. This means that every promise you make, no matter how small, should be kept. If you say you're going to pick your child up from school at a certain time, be sure to do that. If you promise to take your kids to a movie on your day off, by all means, keep your promise. If you promise to let your kids go play in the mud, by golly, let them act like pigs and enjoy the mud; just remember to always keep your word to your child.

So is it possible to always keep every single one of your promises? Of course, it isn't. There will be times that you will have to break your promises, but as long as you commit to doing make-ups with your children, they will definitely understand. Make-up is what you do whenever you have to break a promise to your child. The make-up redevelops trust and lets your children know that they can count on you. This should be done whenever you break a promise, but it should definitely not be abused. Children are very perceptive, and they will immediately recognize when you are breaking your promises too often and using make-ups to cover up your broken promises. Be a man of integrity. Always keep your word.

Step 10.
Lead by example.

Children learn more from what you do than from what you say. Lead by example, and show them how an authentic male acts and behaves. Be sure to exude the four cornerstones of an authentic male in all of your interactions with others. Maintain responsibility, accountability, integrity, and faith. Let them see you smile, and show a passion for life. Let them know that it's all right for them to disagree with you sometimes and to think for themselves. Treat all people with respect and dignity, and by all means, show them that you love their mother even if you're no longer with her. It's important for children to see their fathers develop amicable relationships with their mothers even if they happen to be divorced. Speaking from experience, I can assure you that if you are able to do this, it will pay huge dividends in the long run for you and your children.

If you happen to have male children, be sure to talk to them about the five illusions of manhood. Let them know that it's okay to be a one-woman man and that showing emotions is not a sign of weakness. Let them know that they do not have to constantly compete with other men and that they do not need titles and labels to define who they are. Engage them in a new conversation with men, and let them become a part of this revolution. Remember that you are the leader that they are destined to follow; do not insist that they follow your trail. Give them the choice to choose their own path. You'll be glad you did.

If all men would adhere to these steps, I believe we could eliminate fatherlessness from our society. Of course, this isn't a simple task, but it starts one man at a time, and right now, that one man is you.

My hope is that you will take these lessons and apply them to your life. In doing so, we will begin shifting the consciousness of all the men on the planet. Before you know it, *A New Conversation with Men* will spread across the globe, and the world will never be the same. Fatherlessness will be a thing of the past, and all around the world, men will join our revolution and commit to their own personal transformation.

So I'd like to close this chapter with a challenge to you. If you accept this challenge, I can assure you that you will be doing your part to spread a new conversation with men. Here is your challenge: If you have children that you have not spoken to for a while, make a concerted effort to contact them. Although this may be extremely difficult for you, do it anyway. If you choose to take on this challenge, be aware that this can be frightening to you and your child, and it definitely will not be easy. But feel the fear, and do it anyway. Do not be afraid of how they will react. Simply speak from your heart, and let them know that you were thinking about them and simply wanted to say hello. If appropriate, ask them to forgive you for not contacting them sooner, and let them know whether or not you want to try to reestablish a relationship with them.

If you're not comfortable calling them, write them a letter and tell them how you feel. Let them know just how much you have missed them, and also let them know how hard it may be for you to simply write the letter. If you're struggling with what to say, simply tell them that you were reading this book and decided to follow its advice. You might even use the book as a topic of conversation. Share some of the things you have learned from reading this book. Be honest, open and transparent as much as you can be. Do not criticize or judge them for their responses; simply allow them to express whatever is on their mind.

Do not have any expectations. Just complete the challenge, and see what happens. If it goes well, then reconnect with your children, and make a new commitment to get involved in their lives somehow. If they choose not to speak with you, you haven't really lost anything anyway. Let your heart be your guide, and always put your children's well-being at the forefront of all of your actions.

Be sure to take some time to consider the consequences of your actions. If you are going to try to reestablish a relationship with your child, there are lots of things to consider. For example, ask yourself these questions:

Are you willing to commit time to reconnect with your child if they ask you to?

What if they are in another state and want to see you? What will you do?

What if they want to come and visit you? Are you in a position to make that happen?

Are you currently in a relationship? If so, how would that person feel if you reconnected with your child? Are you able to discuss this openly with them?

How did they react? Are they supportive? Are they against it?

These are just a few of the questions you need to ask yourself before you make contact. Take some time to think about these questions and any others that may come to mind. Then choose what you would like to happen. Once you have made the choice, then simply do whatever it takes to make it happen.

I'd really like to hear your success stories if you decide to do this. So why not log onto our website at www.anewconversationwithmen.com and post a message on our blog or send me an e-mail after you have completed the challenge?

Good luck!

"Be joyful always, pray continually; give thanks in all circumstances, for this is God's will for you in Christ."

— 1 Thessalonians 5:16-18

Chapter Eight

Joy, Passion, and Creativity

After I completed giving a seminar, a gentleman who apparently disagreed with most of what I had said approached me. I could tell by the look on his face that he was obviously unhappy. The topic of discussion was joy, and I knew that this man could not relate to the topic. As he approached me, I knew that I would have to practice what I preached by being friendly and courteous to him. "Hello," I said.

"Hello. I was listening to your topic, and I have to disagree with what you said," stated the angry-looking man.

"What part of the speech did you disagree with?"

"Most of it, actually. I don't think men are supposed to be joyful. Not only are they not supposed to be joyful, I do not think that they are supposed to smile so much. I don't trust a man that smiles so much."

"What is it about a smiling man that you don't trust?"

"I'm not exactly sure, but I know that men who smile so much are usually up to no good. My daddy told me to always look out for men who smile all the time."

"What if your daddy was wrong? What if there are men who smile a lot and are also trustworthy? What if you were one of those men? Do you think it's possible for you to be happy and smile every now and then?"

JOY, PASSION, AND CREATIVITY

"I really don't have any reason to smile. Life is tough, and I think that it's important to be prepared for the worst. That's why I keep my feelings to myself and don't act like a sissy by smiling."

"So you think that smiling makes you less of a man?" "To some degree I do."

"What if you're wrong? What if you could smile and be joyful and still maintain your masculinity?"

"I don't think that's possible, but I'm sure I'm not going to change your point of view. I just wanted to express my opinion. I appreciate you listening. Have a nice day!"

As the angry man walked away, I felt sorry for him. I knew there was a part of him that really wanted to be happy, but I also recognized that he did not have the emotional tools to access his joy. I wanted to embrace him and let him know that he could find his joy if he really wanted to, but I knew that he would not have been receptive to any type of embrace or physical contact.

Our conversation confirmed the need for men to create a new dialog about what it means to be a man in today's ever-changing world. Amazingly, there are millions of men who feel exactly as the angry man felt. They have bought into the illusion that feeling and expressing joy is for women, and that somehow, it makes us less than men if we express our positive emotions. The truth of the matter is, expressing our emotions is our birthright. It isn't feminine to express emotions, and it does not make you a sissy. It takes a lot of courage to be emotionally open and honest in our current paradigm of masculinity. Our country is paying a terrible price for this antiquated way of thinking and behaving, and the time has come to create a new paradigm of masculinity.

In this new paradigm, we learn to connect to our joy and our happiness. We give ourselves permission to be creative and artistic without fear of being labeled "gay" or "feminine." We would also recognize that men who smile all the time could be trustworthy, and that smiling has lots of health benefits, in addition to making you feel good.

So the next time you see a man smiling, don't accuse him of being weak or too sensitive. Recognize that he just might be filled with joy, and the only way he can release it is to smile and be happy. If you are really courageous, walk up to him with a smile on your face and say, "It's really nice to meet a man that is living with joy. I know exactly how you feel, and that is why I have this humongous smile on my face also. I am living with joy, and I absolutely love it!"

So now, it's time for you to answer this question: When was the last time you felt real joy? When I say joy, I'm not talking about being a little happy. I'm talking about the joy you felt when you were a little kid, and it was Christmas morning, and you just opened up that present that you had been praying for all along. Do you remember that joy? How about your first girlfriend? Do you remember that deep-seated-in-your-gut joy that came from your first kiss? Or what about your first car? Do you remember the pride and the joy you felt the first time you drove your very own car all by yourself?

It's that joy that is so deep that there is absolutely no way that you can keep a smile off of your face. It is that ecstatic feeling of aliveness that makes you giggle inside. If you've ever felt this joy, you should actually be smiling right now. Are you?

So when was the last time you felt that joy? Do you remember? Whether you remember it or not, you have experienced joy, and although you may have forgotten how it felt, I can assure you that the joy is still within you. The question you must now ask yourself is whether or not you will allow yourself to feel that joy again and then let it out.

Are you ready? Would you like to know my five steps to accessing your joy? I think you're ready, so here they are:

Heal Your Heart Move into the Silence Practice

Do What You Love

Share Your Joy with Others

1. Healing Your Heart

If it sounds as if I'm repeating myself, I am. But I personally know of no better way to connect with your joy than to heal your heart. If you have unresolved emotional conflict within you, then it will be very difficult to access your joy. If you're holding onto negative emotions, such as anger, resentment, and disappointment, then these emotions will cover up your joy and keep you from accessing it. In order to connect with your joy, you must be able to feel; if you are disconnected from your feelings, how can you expect to feel joy? If you are currently dealing with any type of addiction, it is important to know that you must move past that addiction first in order to feel your joy. Addictions will keep you disconnected from your feelings, and they must be resolved before true, authentic joy can be attained.

If you are looking for ways to heal your heart, go back to Chapter Five and reread the chapter on transformation. If you're looking for other ways, I'd like to share two powerful things you can do right now to help you heal your heart. My first recommendation is to think of someone that you have been angry with over the past year or so. Try to recall what you are angry about, and see if you can recreate the feeling of anger within you. Do you feel it? Can you feel the negative energy in your body? Does the thought of this person cause your blood to boil?

Now ask yourself, is it really worth holding onto this anger? Are there any benefits of keeping this negative energy inside of you? Does your negative energy have any effect on the person you are angry with? Wouldn't you feel better if you could release your anger?

Now, what would happen if you were able to let go of that negative energy? If you released that energy, wouldn't it allow room for some positive energy to replace it? I believe that it will, and if you are willing to do this, I can assure you that you have begun healing your heart and making room for your joy.

Now would be a good time for you to contact that person and forgive them. I promise you that you will feel much better if you do it sincerely. In doing so, you will feel a positive shift in your heart, which opens the door to your joy.

If this is too difficult, you might try bringing up all of the anger and negative energy you feel towards this person, and then write down all of the reasons (separately) you're angry at them on a piece of paper. Next, create a ceremony in which you take all of the things you have written and prepare to place them, one by one into a non-flammable bowl. Take each thing you're angry with and read it out loud with as much anger energy as you feel. After you've expressed the anger, take a deep breath, then tell yourself, "I forgive and release this negative energy." Light the paper with a candle, and watch it burn as you release the negative energy. Drop it into the bowl and move to the next one.

Once you are finished, take a few moments of silence, simply staring at the candle, and notice if you still feel the negative energy. If so, start over and try it again. The more you do this, the more negative energy you will release. Try it; you might like it.

Another word for this exercise is forgiveness. Forgiving someone who has hurt you is a surefire way to heal your heart. The act of forgiveness is never about the other person, it's always for your benefit. It's about your releasing negative energy so that positive energy will have room in your heart. The more positive energy you feel inside, the more joyful you will feel.

I'm reminded of a story I learned from Dr. Wayne Dyer. Dr. Dyer said that most people believe that a person dies from a poisonous snake bite. The fact is, no one actually dies from the bite; they actually die from the poison that is injected into their bodies. Forgiveness is the process of releasing the poison of anger from your body. Although someone may have hurt you, it isn't the initial hurt that kills your joy, it is the poison of anger.

Practice forgiveness, and watch your joy come to the surface.

2. Move into the Silence

If you really want to experience joy, you must learn to quiet your mind and move into silence. Joy is a function of the heart and cannot be experienced through the mind. Learning to quiet your mind and connect to your heart is the foundation of your joy. You cannot think your way to joy; you must feel the joy that is always present.

This is why I am an advocate of meditation. Meditation helped me quiet my mind and connect to my heart. As a result of this practice, I am more peaceful, calm, and centered. It is an integral part of my life, and I can't imagine life without it. You, too, must learn to be still and know that you are connected to the joy that is simply waiting to be expressed.

3. Practice

Have you ever heard that practice makes perfect? This definitely holds true when it comes to joy. It is absolutely critical that you practice, practice, practice expressing your joy. This means that you make a conscious effort to walk your talk and live with joy. This is much easier said than done. The overwhelming majority of men will not be able to do this. Living with joy and expressing it goes completely opposite to what our current male paradigm supports us in doing. Men will attack you, question you, not trust you, and even threaten you if you appear joyful all of the time. This is why it is so important to have a support system to practice your joy with. If you feel moved, I highly recommend that you contact the Mankind Project as a support system. Their web address is www.mkp.org. I promise you that they will support you in your joy while also offering tools to help you access it.

4. Do What You Love

The fact of the matter is this: most people do not know what they love to do! This is because we are conditioned to always focus our attention on material things outside of ourselves (money, positions, stuff) instead of asking ourselves what makes our hearts sing. For example, when choosing a career path, most people ask how much money they will be able to make and then make their decision based on the answer to this question. This choice is based on the premise that money will make you happy. Therefore, the person chooses the job with the highest salary, believing that the more money they make, the happier they will be. This is why so many people are unhappy.

How many people do you know that ask, "What really makes my heart sing, and how can I create a career that allows me to express that?" I can assure you that there are very few people that ask this question. Unfortunately, it isn't until we begin asking ourselves these questions that we can actually find the answers to them. When we are able to ask this very basic question, we are then moving in the direction of happiness and fulfillment. We then open ourselves up to knowing that we should be rich as a result of our happiness rather than being happy as a result of our riches.

I will admit that for most of my life, I've wanted to be an entrepreneur. I have dreamed of this since I was 8 years old. I wanted to be an entrepreneur because I have always believed that it was the only way I could become a billionaire. At the beginning, I wasn't trying to find my life's purpose; I was simply trying to find the surest way for me to become rich. It wasn't until some twenty years later that I found out that I absolutely love running companies, and that being an entrepreneur is part of my life's purpose. Now, I am doing what I love as an extension of my heart's joy, and simply allowing whatever monetary reward I receive to be a result of sharing my passions. In other words, I do what makes my heart sing and detach from the outcome of any monetary reward. The magical part about this is that money just begins to show up in many different forms.

So the key is to discover what you love, and then do it with passion. If you focus your attention on what you love, then I believe that your purpose in life will magically appear through the things you love to do. Since most people have no idea what they love to do, I wanted to share three ways to know if you are doing what you really love.

1. When you are doing what you really love, you do it without the thought of compensation. In other words, you do not do it for money. This does not mean that you can't make money doing it; it simply means that you do it because it makes your heart sing. If you make money with it, you're happy; if you don't make any money, you're still happy.

2. When you are doing what you love, time disappears. This is difficult to explain in words, but when you are doing what you love, you literally have no concept of time. Three hours can feel like three minutes while you are fully engaged in doing what you love. Here's a perfect example: I absolutely love writing and speaking. When I'm writing, I can sit at my computer for hours, and it feels like minutes. The same thing goes for public speaking.

Let me give you a concrete example of how this works for me. Whenever I write, I usually start by spending a few moments in silence, simply quieting my mind. Once I'm relaxed, I simply sit in front of my computer and begin typing. I never make notes or have any type of reference material. I simply move into the silence and allow the ideas to come to me. Before long, a stream of ideas will begin to flow, and before I know it, I've already completed a chapter. It's pretty amazing, actually. Let me share an article I wrote in approximately 15 minutes.

Why are men so uncomfortable watching "Chick Flicks"?

by Michael Taylor

For as long as I can remember, I have always loved movies. As I reflect back on my teenage years, some of my greatest memories include going to the movies. Of course, back then my interest wasn't always focused on the movie. In most cases, I was more interested in using the movie as a way to get my date in a dark, quiet place. If I were really lucky, I might even get a chance to "accidentally" touch her breast as I attempted to put my arm around her. Those were the good old days.

Now that I am happily married and do not have to "accidentally" touch my wife's breast, (another good reason to be happily married), I can really focus my attention on the movies and their content. As I have grown older and become more aware, I have come to the conclusion that movies are really metaphors for life, and if we watch them with an open heart and an open mind, they can assist us in our emotional and spiritual growth.

Steven Simon (author and producer of *Somewhere in Time* and *What Dreams May Come*) really encapsulates how I feel about movies when he writes, "Movies are the most electrifying communications medium ever devised and the natural conduit of inspiring ourselves to look into the eternal issues of who we are and why we are here."

Now, I'm sure most people reading this may not have such a serious definition of what movies mean, but to me, that sums it up. Movies can inspire us and help us discover who we are and why we are here.

I love all genres of movies, sci-fi, action, drama, comedy, you name them; I love them. Like most guys, I have a passion for action films. I enjoy the special effects, the explosions, and of course the ass-kicking martial arts films. I remember watching Bruce Lee in *Enter the Dragon* and being mesmerized by his martial arts. His body was like poetry in motion, and the fact that he was able to fight off 10-20 guys at a time definitely made him a hero in my eyes. As a matter of fact, I think I still have a knot on my head from trying to emulate his moves with my homemade nun chucks. One thing that I like about my wife is that she also loves martial arts films.

She told me that if I had not married her, she was going to marry Jet Li the kung-fu fighting, ass-kicking king of cinema. Good thing I got there before he did.

Now I'm sure most guys may not admit to this, but I also love animated movies. I love them so much that I do not even have to pretend to take my kids to watch them. Of course, my kids are grown up now, so I could not use them as an excuse even if I wanted to, but the truth is, I have absolutely no problem going to the theater and sitting through an animated feature all by myself. There are two reasons why I enjoy animated films. First, it keeps me in touch with my inner child and the feelings of joy that comes from that connection. Second, I really love computer animation and watching how technology continues to evolve and how realistic the animation looks. In my opinion computer animation is an art form. It is a beautiful, creative expression that really moves me.

And now, we get to the real reason I wrote this article. You see, I have a confession to make. I am not embarrassed or ashamed of this, and I do not feel like less of a man by saying this. Are you ready for the confession? Here it is. I love *chick flicks*!

That's right, I love them. Of course, the appropriate term for the genre is "romantic movies," so I will use that term as I share why I enjoy them so much.

I must be honest and tell you that I have not always enjoyed romantic movies. I was like most men; they would make me extremely uncomfortable because I did not know how to express my feelings as I watched them. If ever I felt emotional, I would repress the feelings and not allow myself to experience the appropriate emotion. Like most men, I was unable to be open and vulnerable enough to deflect the emotion with some unconscious attempt to not appear too sensitive. My defense mechanism of choice was laughter. If ever I would become overwhelmed with sadness, I would crack a joke to deflect the feeling. If I were overcome with joy and happiness, I would simply laugh in an inauthentic manner to keep from feeling true joy. Whenever I feel deep joy, I usually cry, and that was a huge blow to my masculine ego, so I never allowed that to happen. So rather than expose myself to the possibility of being emotional, I used to avoid romantic movies like I avoided rectal exams.

But now, things are different. As a result of my healing and inner work, I am able to experience movies at a deep, emotional level. I can now allow myself the freedom to simply experience whatever emotion I'm feeling and then express whatever feeling I'm having spontaneously and authentically. It amazes me how much of the movies

I used to miss because I did not allow myself to feel and experience the movie. Now that I am open to all of my emotions, it simply makes the movie-going experience more enjoyable.

This is just one of many benefits of doing inner work and connecting to your emotions. Movies have more meaning; your sense of beauty is heightened, relationships are more rewarding and fulfilling, your spirituality is deeper and more connected, and your sense of self is elevated.

So if you happen to be one of those guys that are afraid of watching chick flicks, ask yourself these questions:

Are you uncomfortable expressing your emotions?

Are you afraid of watching a chick flick because you might not be able to hold back the tears of sadness or joy?

Are you so insecure in your masculinity that you simply refuse to even consider checking out a chick flick?

Are you afraid of being called a punk, wimp, or sissy?

Whatever your reason for avoiding chick flicks, just accept the fact that it does not make you less of a man by viewing a movie. Know that real men are comfortable with their emotions and have no difficulty expressing them. And last but not least, it's okay to cry.

Ponder on this for a while, and let me know what you think. In the meantime, I've got a hot date with my wife to watch a chick flick. If I'm lucky, I might get that opportunity to accidentally let my hand touch her breast. I'm so excited! See you at the movies!

The reason that I'm able to write so quickly is because of my love of writing. In addition, the reason that the article was so easy to write is because I was writing about something that I absolutely love, movies! Whenever you do something out of joy and passion versus duty and obligation, I can assure you that you will be much more effective at it, and it will definitely be a lot easier to do.

This is the reason that you must discover the things that you love to do. When you connect to that which makes your heart sing, I believe you are tapping into the Infinite Intelligence that created the universe, and you then become a conduit through which the universe expresses itself. Take Marsha Sinetar's advice. "Do what you love; the money will follow!"

3. *When you are doing what you love, you want to share it with others.* When you are truly doing what you love, I can promise you that you will want to share it with others. No matter what it is, sharing your talents with others is another way of making your heart sing. The amazing thing is that when you are sharing your gifts with others. not only do you get a chance to express your passions, you also give others the opportunity to share them as well. While you are sharing, and they are receiving, your heart begins exploding with joy. That's why the line, "Love isn't love until you give it away," is so important. When you are doing what you love, give it away!

When you take all five steps to accessing your joy, you will barely be able to contain yourself. You will begin feeling an overflowing of joy that you have to release. The beauty of it is that the more you give, the more you will have to give. Your joy is infinite. You cannot run out of it. By sharing your joy with others, you give other people the courage and the freedom to express their own.

Here's a quick test for you. Take a moment and list 10 things that you love to do. (Remember the three ways to know when you are doing what you love?)

1. _____
2. _____
3. _____
4. _____
5. _____
6. _____
7. _____
8. _____
9. _____
10. _____

Were you able to list 10? Was it easy or hard for you to complete the list? As you look at your list, try to determine which are the five most important to you. Now separate those onto a new list. Take the items from this list and make a commitment to yourself that you will do all five of them within the next couple of weeks. As you do these things, try to recognize which one brings you the most joy. Once you can figure out the one that "lights you up", you are on the right path to finding what you love to do. You should then participate in whatever this is for you, and do it because you love it, not because you're trying to make money at it. Keep doing this thing, and see if the joy stays with you; if it doesn't, try something else from your list.

Once you find the one that feels right, you will then have to figure out if this is something you would like to pursue as a career path. If it is, you will then have to figure out how to pursue this path and then attract the money necessary to make a living. If you will first find the thing that really brings you joy, I can assure you that the means to do this will show up in unexpected ways. Be sure to do your due diligence, and don't make any quick irrational decisions. Trust the little nudges received from within, and let them guide you the rest of the way.

Here is one of the first list of things I love to do that I came up with several years ago.

1. Reading books
2. Having deep, stimulating conversations
3. Using computers
4. Managing people
5. Teaching
6. Going to the movies
7. Learning new things
8. Traveling
9. Working out
10. Being an entrepreneur

When I wrote this list, I had no idea that one day, I would become a radio-show host and author. I simply knew that I loved doing these things. By loving to engage in deep, stimulating conversations, my radio show was born. By loving books, I became an author. By loving to teach, I became a personal development coach and motivational speaker. By doing the things that bring me joy, I have connected with my passions, which allows me to live my dreams. If I can do it, so can you. You simply have to believe that it's possible and put one foot in front of the other until you finally reach your dream.

If you're looking for a great resource to help you discover your passions, I highly recommend that you pick up a copy of *The Passion Test* by Janet Bray Attwood and Chris Attwood. It is a step-by-step guide to assist you in discovering the things you are most passionate about. Check it out and find your passions.

It's important that you take the time to write down the things you love; when you do, divine providence steps in, and before you know it, doors will begin opening for you in ways you could never have imagined. But if you refuse to take the first step, then you will remain stuck in the same place doing the same thing that you know does not bring you joy. Aren't you ready for something different?

"I believe deeply that we must find, all of us together, a new spirituality. We need a new concept, a lay spirituality. We ought to promote this concept with the help of scientists. It could lead us to set up what we are all looking for—a secular morality."

—Dalai Lama, Spiritual Leader of Tibetan Buddhism, from

Violence and Compassion: Conversations with the Dalai Lama

Chapter Nine

Spirituality

There is a very small part of me that really does not want to write this chapter. That part of me knows that more people have died in the name of God than for any other reason. That small part of me also knows that most people are very closed-minded about God and therefore end up having arguments and disagreements about God that cause hatred, separation, and sometimes even death. Families, communities, and even countries have been divided and destroyed because of a person's need to be right about their beliefs about God, and the last thing I want to do is to create that sort of division and violence in the world.

That part of me also realizes that I do not have a degree in theology or philosophy. I am not a minister or an expert, and some people may argue that I do not have the right to write about God. I realize that people will judge, attack, and criticize and even condemn my point of view, so wouldn't it be easier just to skip this chapter and forego any negative response? Shouldn't I just keep my point of view about God to myself and avoid any unnecessary conflict?

Should I risk the condemnation, ridicule, and attack of the critics and men of the cloth who will claim to be the experts and know-it-alls of religion? Will I be able to defend and explain how I came to the conclusions about God that I write about in this chapter?

As I ponder the latter questions, the answer bursts forth from my heart so loudly that I can barely contain it. The answer is an emphatic, YES! Not only should I write this chapter, but I should write this chapter with all the passion and joy that I feel in my heart as a result of my relationship with my creator. I must sing from the mountaintops of the God of my understanding that has filled my life with joy, abundance, and inner peace. I must share the lessons I've learned and dispel some of the negative beliefs about God that have been passed down for generations. In other words, I believe it's time for a new conversation about God.

As I mentioned earlier, my intention is not to cause any division or arguments about God. I do not claim to be an expert, and I realize that I will be sharing my truth and my truth only. There is a distinct possibility that my truth may be different from your truth. My hope is that you will be open-minded enough to simply examine your truth and be open to a new perspective about God. If you find yourself agreeing or disagreeing with my point of view, simply listen to your own inner voice and decide which works best for you. There is ultimately only one truth, the only truth that matters is your truth. So as you're reading this chapter, tune into your truth, and see if the message in my words speaks to you. If not, simply hold on to your own truth, and then live your life as a demonstration of your faith.

Before I share my story, I would like to share a couple of statistics from a recent report put out by the Pew Forum on Religion & Public Life. The report stated that 28% of American adults have left the faith in which they were raised in favor of another religion or no religion at all. It also stated that men are significantly more likely to claim no religious affiliation. It said that nearly one in five men say they have no formal religious affiliation, compared with roughly 13% of women. This is the statistic that really stood out for me. As you read through this chapter, you may find out why so many men stay away from religion.

It was a thought-provoking and interesting report, but what really intrigued me was the reaction from a large percentage of ministers and clergy around the country. Their immediate reaction was to use this report to talk about the moral decline in America. They began using this report to explain why there is so much violence and hatred in our country. Their argument was that if more people went to church, then we would not have as much crime and hatred in our society. They argued that the reason our schools were in such decay was that we had taken God out of the classrooms, and this was God's way of punishing our country. A lot of the ministers used this report as a scare tactic to get people to go to church and to promote their belief that the world was spiraling downward, out of control, and the only way to save our country was to repent our sins and surrender to God.

So what do you think? Do you think the ministers were right? Is our country in the midst of a moral and ethical decline? Is God really punishing us for taking religion out of the schools? If everyone went to church, would it solve all of this country's problems?

These are big questions with no small answers. Although I do not claim to have all the answers, I would like to share my interpretations of the report from the Pew Forum on Religion & Public Life.

It is my fervent belief that the report is actually a signal that most people are simply disenchanted with organized religion. This does not mean that they have given up on God: it simply means that they are searching for a different type of connection to God. Although this report may appear to say that we're becoming less religious, what it does not report is that more and more people are finding other ways to nurture their spirits. More and more people are becoming spiritual versus religious, and it would be difficult to include this in any report. There are some people (me included) who believe that we are actually in the midst of creating a new spirituality. This new spirituality creates a whole new paradigm of participating with the divine. I believe that the old fire-and-brimstone teaching of the past is giving way to a new intimacy and connection with God never before experienced. This new spirituality teaches us that we can have God without religion, and we do not have to embrace antiquated theologies and belief systems that do not align with our own inner truth. It's been called the Great Shift or Great Awakening by some and the Evolution of Consciousness by others. But no matter what you call it, I believe something deeply spiritual and transformational is occurring on our planet.

Instead of trying to preach to you or sway your point of view, I would simply like to share my own personal story about my search for God. This will be a condensed version because I do not have room to place the entire story in a single chapter. As a matter of fact, I will be writing a new book that chronicles my search for God titled, *Knock! Knock! Who's There? It's Me, GOD!* This book will share my entire journey to find the God of my understanding, and it should be released in the very near future. Stay tuned; you will not want to miss it.

So now, I would like to share the condensed version of how I found the God of my understanding. As stated earlier, be sure to try to keep an open mind. Try not to let your current beliefs keep you from receiving some new insights. Remember this quote: "The mind is like a parachute; it only works when it is open." Keep your mind open! Let's begin.

As mentioned in previous chapters, back in 1990, I had reached the lowest point in my life. I had gone through a divorce, bankruptcy, and foreclosure, and I had recently quit my job to try to start my own company. Everything in my life seemed to be going wrong. As a result, I had fallen into a deep state of depression, and I could hardly function on any level.

I was desperate and alone, and I needed help and support, but I did not know where to turn. Late one night, I was watching television, and I happened to turn on one of those 24-hour religious channels. As I listened, I unknowingly began praying that the minister would say something that would help me feel a little better. As I listened to this minister, his message began to seep into my mind, and all of a sudden, I had a sense of hope. The minister said that no matter how bad our lives may seem or no matter how dark the world could be, there was always someone we could count on to turn that darkness into light. He said that this person could take your burdens away and could love you back to wholeness. The person's name was Jesus, and He was available to you right now. All you had to do was accept Him as your Lord and Savior, and you would be lifted up and forgiven and be able to start your life anew.

As I sat there staring at the television, I began wondering if this were really true. Could Jesus really help me turn my life around? Could He remove all of the pain and shame I was feeling in my heart? Was it really possible for me to turn my life around and start all over again?

As I sit here now, almost twenty years later thinking in retrospect, I remember this moment as though it were yesterday. I specifically remember placing my hand on the television set and praying to Jesus to come into my life and to remove all of my pain. I remember listening to the minister say that no matter how far you've fallen, you can always get back up, but you must reach out to Jesus to assist you. So I stuck out my hand, placed it on the television screen, and cried out, "Jesus, I accept You as my Lord and Savior, and I ask You to come into my heart. Please help me!"

As I cried out in desperation, something in me shifted. All of a sudden, my world didn't seem so dark. For the first time in a very long time, I actually smiled. I had a sense of hope, and I felt as if my life had definitely taken a turn for the better. I watched the programming for several hours and eventually fell asleep. When I woke up the next morning, I knew I needed to go to church so that I could maintain this new sense of hope in my heart.

Since I was brought up Baptist, I decided to stick with that which was most familiar. I had a friend who had been trying to get me to come to his church for a very long time, so I contacted him and asked if I was still welcome. He assured me that I was and gave me the address and meeting times of his church.

The first Sunday that I went to church was amazing. I'm not sure if I was just happy for not being so isolated, or if it was the Holy Spirit in me, but I felt a deep sense of relief and connection as I stepped into the church for the first time in a long time. As the preacher gave the congregation the opportunity to come up to the front of the church to receive Jesus as their Lord and Savior, I immediately got up and took my place at the altar. When the minister asked if I had anything I'd like to share, I told him about my experience watching the late-night religious broadcast, and I shared how in that moment, I believed that Jesus had entered my heart. As I shared my "testimony", I noticed several people in the pews who were so moved by my sharing that they were actually in tears. When I finished speaking, I actually received a standing ovation. It felt really good to be acknowledged in that way, and I felt accepted and loved unconditionally. In that moment, all of my challenges were temporarily set aside, and I no longer felt as if I had to face the world alone.

Needless to say, I joined the church and became very active. I would go to church three or four times a week and found myself participating in several different ministries throughout the church. This continued for several months, and although my financial and personal life were still in shambles, I now had a place to help relieve some of the pressure of those challenges.

My newfound "home" really helped me move through my depression and isolation. Going to church put me back in contact with other people, and that really helped me move through a lot of the loneliness and emptiness I had been feeling for months. I eventually realized that this is what I was craving more than anything: connecting with people and having someone to talk to.

Although I now had a place to talk with other people, I realized that the overwhelming majority of conversations at church were about God or religion. Although these were important topics since I was in a church, I actually wanted to talk about more personal issues. I really wanted to talk openly about the pain of my divorce or the humiliation I felt as a result of my foreclosure and bankruptcy. But I didn't really feel comfortable bringing up these personal issues in the church. I was also afraid that if I did bring up these issues, the only thing that they would tell me to do was to pray about it, and I definitely didn't want to hear that. So I kept my personal issues to myself.

There were definitely lots of benefits I received from going to church, but there were also lots of reasons that I didn't want to go. I started to long for something else, something deeper, something that I had not received from the church, something that would answer all of the questions that I had been too afraid to ask.

Before long, I could no longer deny the fact that I was really having a difficult time believing some of the things they were teaching in the church. Something in me just didn't feel right. I started to feel like a hypocrite because I was agreeing with things that I really didn't believe. All of my doubts and skepticism that I had previously held about religion had now begun to resurface, and I could no longer deny it. I had to face my doubts head on and come to a decision about whether I should stay a member of the church.

Late one night, I started to write down all of the reasons that I should either stay with the church or leave. As I compiled my list, there was one question that stood out as the granddaddy of all questions. I knew that by answering this one question, I would be able to decide which direction I would go.

The question was, Does a physical place called hell really exist? Was there a real physical place that God condemned people to go to if they didn't believe in Him and obey His commandments? This was the question that I needed an answer to because it was the one that I truly couldn't understand and accept.

Why would a loving God need to condemn the children He loves to eternal hell? If He was that angry, why not simply banish them from heaven and let their souls float aimlessly around the universe or something? Or why not give them different time limits in hell based on the severity of their sins? Shouldn't a person who goes to hell for simply saying he doesn't believe in God have a shorter sentence in hell than a mass murderer? This made sense to me, but it still didn't answer my initial questions.

How could a God of love be so cruel and vindictive? What would be the point of this eternal damnation? If God truly loved us, wouldn't He have come up with something a little more humane? This question had bothered me my entire life, and now I knew that I needed to face it head-on and come to my own truth and understanding about it.

As I sat there pondering this question, I intuitively knew I did not believe that there was a literal place called hell. And since I didn't believe in hell, how could I or why should I believe in God? In that moment, I decided to stop believing in God. I made a conscious choice based on my own gut feelings that God really didn't exist.

The next day, I called my minister and set up an appointment to meet with him. At our meeting, I told him how I honestly felt and what I truly believed. I told him that I would not be returning to his church, but I appreciated everything he had done for me as a pastor. His response didn't surprise me. He told me that I would end up in hell and live there for eternity. He didn't say it with any vengeance or malice, but I knew that he really believed what he said.

Fortunately for me, I truly didn't believe what he said. Therefore, I was 100% comfortable with my decision and would accept the consequences of my actions. If he was right, I would accept the consequences, and if I was right, I would accept my death on my terms with no fear. Either way, I felt completely comfortable with my decision and choice to leave the church.

During this time, I had begun dealing with some of my personal issues by going to therapy and participating in personal-development workshops. As I continued to heal my heart and expand my mind, I actually concluded that all of my pain and suffering were the result of my tragic childhood. By healing my childhood wounds, I could remove the pain and ultimately be free. As a result of my participation in healing my emotions, I began to learn to feel again, and it helped me heal all types of relationships. I found my joy again as a result of my healing. I also begin learning how to create intimacy in my relationships, and my social life began to flourish. The analytical part of me concluded that this was the key to my success, and there was no need for God in any shape form or fashion. I reconfirmed my belief that there was no such thing as God, and I officially began calling myself an atheist.

As an atheist, I decided that all of man's pain and suffering could be resolved through logic and science. This new acceptance and understanding challenged me to begin studying psychology, the new quantum physics, and science, and it really felt right for me at the time. I studied some of the work of Carl Jung and Sigmund Freud and learned how the subconscious mind and the ego function and operate. I took a completely scientific view of the world and felt that the intellect was the key to solving any problem. This worked extremely well for me for approximately three years. But there was something missing. Although I was experiencing joy, happiness and serenity, I still felt incomplete. It was as if I had completed this beautiful 500-piece puzzle and only one of the pieces was missing. No matter how beautiful it was, it still wasn't complete without that last piece. I needed to find that last piece.

So I began to ask myself some much deeper questions. Questions like, "Why am I here? What is my purpose? What is the meaning of life? These questions challenged me to go much deeper than the intellect could go, so I had to be willing to take my questioning to a whole different level. Ultimately, it came back to life's single most important question: "Is there really a God?"

Since I had already concluded that God did not exist, I was hesitant to ask myself this question. Therefore, it was extremely difficult for me to move to this level of questioning. There was a part of me that was adamant about not believing in God, and there was the other part of me that had to find that missing piece to my life's puzzle.

To appease both parts of myself, I decided that I would go on a journey to prove to myself that God did not exist. This Ultimately, I would satisfy both sides of myself, which I believed would put my mind and heart at ease. By going on this journey, I did not have to say I believed in God, and at the same time, I did not have to say that I didn't. But this way, I knew that I could come to a final conclusion that I could believe in and live with.

To begin my journey, I decided that I would try something other than a Baptist church. I concluded that maybe it was simply the Baptist's teaching that my heart disagreed with. By trying other faiths, maybe I would come to a different conclusion. I decided to try the Methodist church, the Pentecostal church and the Catholic church to find a place that worked for me. I attended each one and asked very deep questions about their beliefs and traditions. I spent time with the leaders of these churches and would ask them not only what they personally believed, but why they believed it. Each of the leaders was easy to talk with and did not try to convince me to join their church. They actually applauded me for my willingness to ask deeper questions and said that they hoped that I found whatever it was that I was looking for. Unfortunately, none of them felt right. I was definitely still struggling with the concept of hell, and none of these belief systems were really any different than my Baptist teaching. I had to continue my journey.

I then decided to research the origin of the Bible. I wanted to know what made this book so special, and more importantly, why should I believe it. As I researched the origins, I came to several new and exciting conclusions. As a result of my research, I concluded that I had always been taught that the Bible was supposed to be taken literally. What I learned was that this was incorrect. I came to the understanding that the Bible is really a series of stories and allegories that should actually be interpreted metaphysically. What that means is that the people and stories in the Bible are actually symbolic of, and metaphors for our current life experiences. In other words, when I can understand the deeper meaning in the stories and how the characters are actually different aspects of myself, then I am interpreting the Bible from a metaphysical or spiritual point of view. This makes all of the stories in the Bible practical and relevant to my current life experiences. This interpretation brings the Bible to life and then provides me with insights and wisdom, which can help me solve any number of personal challenges that I may be dealing with.

I also concluded that the Bible is not the only revelation from God. Every great religious text comes from the same source. People call this source God, Allah, Yahweh, Jehovah, Krishna, Buddha, Mohammed, or Spirit. But ultimately, each word that we use to try to describe the indescribable is simply a metaphor or symbol that we use to try to comprehend the incomprehensible.

When we embrace this fundamental truth, we can then choose the path that is right for us. Once we choose our path, we must then ask ourselves whether we truly believe what that path teaches us. If that truth aligns with our spirit, then we must incorporate its teachings into our lives. In other words, there are many paths to God, and just because someone may be on a different path from yours does not mean that they are lost. You must choose your own path and accept the revelations of that path. Once you find the path that works for you, embrace it with your heart, mind, and spirit, and let it be your guide.

As a result of my research on the Bible and other spiritual teachings, I then decided that I wanted to move away from the Christian teaching and become open to other philosophies. I then began researching the other major religions of the world, including Hinduism, Islam, Buddhism, and Judaism. This exploration gave me some unique perspectives and opened my mind to other ways of viewing God and the world as a whole. I became a much better human being as a result of this spiritual questioning and examination.

Of all the religions I studied, I felt the deepest connection to the Buddhist teaching. I had been practicing meditation for several years to assist me with relaxation, and the Buddhist teaching helped me deepen my meditation practice. It was in learning to quiet my mind and listen to the still voice within me, that I really begin to "feel" a spiritual connection. What I really liked about the Buddhist teachings was that they put their focus on challenging me to think for myself without telling me that I had to adhere to any religious dogma or teaching. I had the freedom to think for myself, and it was my responsibility to remove any suffering from my own life. Nowhere in the teaching did I hear that I was a sinner or a flawed human being that had to repent of my sins in order to get into heaven. Heaven was a state of consciousness or awareness that I had access to at any time. I did not have to die to go to heaven; I simply had to come to the awareness that I was actually already there. The teaching taught me to always look within myself for my answers and to not depend on experts or gurus to make choices for me. The goal was to attain Buddha Consciousness, and this would only be achieved by removing all negative thoughts, ideas, and perceptions about myself and the world around me from my mind. By emptying my mind of these negative thoughts, I would eventually remove all suffering from my life. This takes commitment, discipline, patience, and faith, but once experienced, it will place you in a state of enlightenment. I embraced the Buddhist philosophies for several years without labeling myself a Buddhist. Another thing that I really like about the religion is that it taught me not to be attached to labels and external titles. By embracing the teachings without attaching myself to labels, I moved into a sense of oneness and connection with the Source of all of life. I learned to feel "spirituality" from the core of my being, and it gave me a deep respect and appreciation for all of life and its creatures.

After several years of personal growth and deepening my spirituality, I begin answering the question that, yes, there really was a God. Although I still had not experienced any irrefutable proof of God's existence, I begin to know for myself that God was real. I remember hoping at times that God would show up in some physical tangible form that would remove any doubt from my mind, but that never happened. Despite this, I begin to know that God was real, and I was connected to this Source in ways that I never imagined possible before. The main lesson I learned through all of this, was that God is not some old white guy sitting up in the clouds taking notes of my life waiting for me to make a mistake. As a matter of fact, God is more of a "what" than a "who." I concluded that God is the divine intelligence that permeates this universe. It is the intelligence in you that makes your heart beat and your blood flow. It is that amazing intelligence that knows how to heal broken bones as well as broken hearts. It is the source of all inspiration and creativity, and everyone has direct access to this divine Source. As I mentioned earlier, God is the Source of all things and goes by many names. It really doesn't matter "what" you call it; it's just important that you are willing to call it.

As a result of these new understandings, I became extremely open to all religions. Each one taught me something new and different about who I am and how I fit into this divine plan called being human. As I continued to learn from these religions, I began asking myself the question about how Jesus fits into the picture called my life. I remembered how I had sat up late that night and convinced myself that I was giving my life over to Jesus. I remembered that feeling of hope that came over me as I surrendered my heart to this very special teacher. There was a part of me that still felt incomplete and somehow I believed that Jesus was the key that would open the door to my completion.

SPIRITUALITY

While sitting up late one night, something in me told me to go and purchase a Bible. It was as if this still small voice in my soul was guiding me to a new revelation or something. I had never purchased a Bible before, and although I had studied the book for the past few years, there were still unanswered questions I needed to find answers to. So I got up and went to a late-night bookstore and purchased one. I bought one of the Bibles in ordinary language because I remembered how confusing the old King James version was to me. I had decided that I was now going to read the Bible for my own understanding so that I could come to my own conclusions about the message and the messenger in this important spiritual document.

Since I had done some previous research on the Bible, I had a pretty good understanding of how it came about. The truth of the matter was that I had actually never read the New Testament for myself, especially the parts where Jesus spoke. So I sat down and decided that I was going to study His teachings and come to my own conclusions about His message.

I must admit that I felt very uncomfortable at the beginning. A part of me was afraid that maybe Jesus wouldn't accept me because I had initially rejected Him. Another part of me was afraid that the Bible wouldn't be relevant to me because of my reading other books about other religions. But because I had purchased my own Bible, and maybe because I was reading it to gain understanding rather than debate its validity, my mind and my heart were wide open. As a result of this, something magical happened. As I begin to read the words of Jesus, it was as if He was sitting right next to me sharing His message. As I continued to read His words, His message penetrated my heart and my spirit, and it overwhelmed me with a deep feeling of love.

The more I read His words, the more my heart opened. Pretty soon, I was crying uncontrollably with the beauty of His teachings. For the next few hours, I read His words and cried with joy. I was absolutely overwhelmed by the feeling of love and connection I was experiencing.

As I continued to read, I realized that I was crying because for the first time in my life, I was actually feeling the love of God. This was the irrefutable proof that I had been looking for all my life, and it confirmed for me that God was real. There is absolutely no way that I could put this feeling into words, but I knew that this was the love that transcends human understanding that the Bible talks about in so many different ways.

I also realized that I was no longer stuck in my intellect; I was now connected to my heart, and that is what allowed me to truly experience this love. I had not experienced this love before because you cannot "feel" love in your head. You must experience it in your heart, and that is exactly what I was doing.

After all of the years of research and exploration, I had finally found the key that opened the door to my connection to God. I had to be willing to get out of my head and into my heart. By uncovering this divine truth, I had come full circle and was now intimately connected to the God of my understanding. I now had all the proof I needed to know that God is real.

To confirm this, I had the most amazing dream. In this dream, I was standing on a precipice of some sort that had a very dark and seemingly endless bottom. As I stood on this precipice looking down, I was filled with this bone-chilling fear. There was a part of me that knew I was supposed to jump, but there was the other part of me that said absolutely not. As I leaned over the edge, I couldn't see anything. I had no idea how deep it was, and I had no idea why I was supposed to jump. But something in me kept nudging and telling me that this is what I was supposed to do. As I stood there in paralyzing fear, I heard a voiceless voice say, "Trust me."

I looked around and did not see anyone.

After a few minutes, I heard the voice again. "Trust me."

"Who are you?" I responded. But there was no answer to that question. "Trust me," the voice said again.

Although I did not understand why, I knew that I was supposed to jump. In the dream, I did not feel depressed or lonely, and I wasn't contemplating suicide, I felt more like I was simply looking for something new and different in my life. Standing on that edge seemed to symbolize taking a leap of faith into the unknown that would eventually lead to that new and different life I was so desperately seeking.

After several moments of different, I gained the courage and decided to jump. When I did, I was filled with fear that I would have never imagined. Although it was just a dream, I still remember the feeling of absolute terror as I began free-falling into the darkness. I remember screaming loudly with fear and swinging my arms and legs frantically in the dark, trying to stop my descent. I was sweating profusely and crying uncontrollably. I honestly believed that I was falling to my death.

After several seconds of freefalling, I heard the voice again. "Trust me." "Who are you?" I screamed. "Why should I trust you? I can't see you, so how am I supposed to trust you?" "Trust me," said the voice.

"Can you help me? Can you stop me from falling? I don't want to die; can you save me?"

Once again the voice said, "Trust me."

By now I was so consumed with fear that I thought my heart would stop. I was still freefalling into this deep abyss of darkness, which I thought would become my permanent resting place.

All of a sudden, I began seeing pictures in my mind of the people I cared about the most. I saw my kids, my wife, my mom, my friends and even some old co-workers whom I hadn't thought about in years. As I watched these pictures flow across my mind, I noticed that my fear was beginning to subside. I was no longer screaming and trying to reach for something to cling to. Before I knew it, the fear went away. I was now freefalling in peace, still with the thought that I was still going to die, but I might as well accept it.

Then the voice returned, "Trust me."

"Who are you? Just tell me your name. I know you can hear me, so would you please just tell me who and what you are?"

There was no answer. After a few more moments of falling, I noticed that I had begun to slow down. In addition to slowing down, I also noticed that there was something that had begun supporting me. I was being embraced by something invisible and non-detectable with my senses, but I definitely had this feeling of being supported by something.

As I continued my descent, my fear completely disappeared. I knew that I was being embraced by some presence, and this presence was now controlling my fall. Before long, my fear turned to happiness, and that happiness was transformed into the deepest level of joy I could ever have imagined. I began crying again, but this time it wasn't out of fear; it was love.

As I looked below me, I noticed a small glimpse of light. As I continued my descent, the light expanded. Before long, there was a brilliant burst of light, which temporarily blinded me. When I was able to see again, I found myself falling into the most beautiful wooded area you could ever imagine. As I stared at its beauty, I prepared myself to brace for the landing.

I was only a few hundred feet from the ground, and I knew that this presence was about to set me on the ground. As my feet touched the ground, I felt the presence release me. As it did, I heard the voice again. "Trust me." "But who are you? Why won't you answer me? I want to thank you for saving me. How do I thank you? "Trust me."

After these words, I woke up from the dream. The dream was so real that even after I had awakened, I was still enveloped in a deep feeling of love and connection. I still felt as if I were in that beautiful wooded area embraced by that loving presence. I sat in bed and cried for several minutes.

After a while, I began deciphering the dream. It immediately made sense to me. I came to the understanding that standing on the edge of the precipice symbolized the leap of faith I took by not accepting the religion of my youth and going on my own personal search for God. The dark represented the unknown, and my willingness to step into it, not knowing where I would end up. The absolute fear represented how I had felt most of my life as a result of not having a connection to the Divine. Seeing the faces of the people I loved meant that I should not be attached to material things. I should understand that what truly gives my life meaning is the love that I received from the important people in my life. The initial burst of light that I saw represented my awakening to my spirituality. The blinding burst of light represented my acceptance of the fact that there really is a God. The beautiful peaceful place in the woods represented the divine love of God that is all around me at all times if I will simply take a leap of faith to connect to it. And the voiceless voice of God saying, "Trust me," symbolizes that God is with me always in every situation. When I "Let go and let God," I will always be embraced by the loving peace and protection of the God of my understanding.

After that experience, I was introduced to Unity Church of Christianity which taught me an entirely different approach to Jesus and His teachings. I learned that Christianity is actually a way of being and living my life. Instead of being attached to the label "Christian," I simply make a conscious effort to be "Christ-like" in all of my interactions with others. This means that I demonstrate all of the qualities and attributes that Jesus demonstrated. Things like forgiveness, non-judgmentalness, compassion, empathy, and most of all, love are all qualities that He came to Earth to teach. By incorporating these qualities into my daily interactions, then I am living a Christ-like life, and that is all that is required of me as a human being.

I also learned that even though Christianity is the foundation of my spirituality, I can still gain insights and wisdom from other spiritual traditions and leaders. As a result of this understanding, I can now go to any church or participate in any religion and still feel completely comfortable. I no longer feel that I will be punished or condemned to hell by learning from Buddha, Krishna, Mohammed, or any other spiritual master. I have the freedom to make my own choices without fear of being banished to some illusionary and fictitious place of eternal damnation and torment.

I have also come to know that there are current spiritual masters who are alive today and are sharing divine truths that help me deepen my spirituality, and they are shining their light on humanity. These modern-day spiritual leaders are the catalyst for the New Spirituality that I believe this country and our world so desperately need. In my own small way, I would like to think of myself as one of these people, people who are not preaching and claiming to have all of the answers, but instead, people who are simply sharing their insights and wisdom with others to help guide them to their own truth and understanding. This is the foundation of the New Spirituality, being a light in an apparently dark world and spreading the light with others.

Back in 1995, I described God this way:

It is my belief that God is like Coke, it's the "Real Thing." Now, some people drink Coke out of a can, and some drink it out of a bottle; others drink it out of chilled glasses, others drink it from plastic containers, while others refuse to drink it at all. But ultimately, the container that it's in really doesn't matter; the only thing that matters is quenching your thirst with the Coke. Religion is the container that holds God, and though the containers may be different, they all hold the same thing. That thing is God, and it is the only thing that can quench your spiritual thirst. It is up to you to choose the container that best suits you.

This is still my favorite explanation of how I see God.

I wanted to share this condensed story of my journey to find my spiritual connection to challenge you to think about your own spiritual life. As mentioned in the Pew report, a large percentage of men do not have any religious affiliation. I believe it is because most of us are disconnected from our hearts, and we try to analyze and rationalize the divine. The fact is, having faith and believing in God is actually pretty irrational if you think about it. It literally does not make sense in a lot of ways. Everything in your mind will convince you that God isn't real, so you must be willing to be "out of your mind" to truly connect to God.

You must be out of your mind and into your heart if you ever want to experience the unconditional love of God.

This is the purpose of *A New Conversation with Men*, to challenge you to look within and come to your own understanding of God and the divine. If you choose to heal your heart and find your own truth, I can assure you that this love is available to you. But you must remember, "Seek and you shall find; knock and the door will be opened to you."

One of my favorite spiritual quotes is this, "Who I am is God's gift to me, what I make of myself is my gift to God." My commitment is to become the very best human being I can become and then help others do the same. This is the way that I say, "Thank you, God," for this wonderful gift called life. By maintaining an attitude of gratitude, and committing myself to be in service to my creator, I am expressing thanks and gratitude to the Source of all things. It is my gift back to God.

I want to close this chapter with my own definition of spirituality. Several years ago I attended a seminar, and the facilitator challenged all of the participants to write their own definitions. He said by coming up with your own definition of spirituality, you would lay the foundation for your spiritual transformation. I spent a lot of time thinking about this and here is the definition I came up with. See if it resonates with you, and if so, incorporate it into your life.

"Spirituality is the moment-to-moment recognition and acknowledgment of my connection to something greater than myself." By embracing this definition, I know that I am connected to my Source at all times. By having this awareness, I am able to see God and beauty in every situation in my life. There is no place and no situation where God is not there for me. This is a very comforting feeling and the foundation of my faith. I hope it touches your spirit and leads you to your own definition and spiritual transformation.

Peace!

"Man who says it cannot be done should get out of the way of man who is doing."

— Chinese proverb

Chapter Ten

The Revolution

Albert Einstein once stated that one of the most important decisions that a person has to make is to decide whether or not we live in a friendly universe. This statement implies that we have a choice, and I believe that this choice will ultimately create your experience of life. In other words, if you believe that the universe is friendly I can assure you that your experience of life will reflect that belief. On the other hand, if you believe that the universe is unfriendly the same rule applies, and you will have those types of experiences.

Some people believe that the world is in total chaos and headed towards a path of destruction. To support their beliefs, they will turn to the media to provide evidence to support their beliefs. They will point to things like the war in Iraq and all the senseless killings in the Middle East. They will show you pictures and tell you stories of child molesters, drug abusers, corporate corruption, and a downward-spiraling economy. They will remind you of all the racial prejudices and inequalities in the world and then show you pictures of emaciated babies starving around the world to confirm the high rates of poverty around the globe. In order to prove their point and validate their positions, they will then bring out the heavy artillery by showing you the statistics from the experts that support their beliefs. (Nothing causes more fear in a person's mind than negative statistics.) Last, they will give the religious pundits the opportunity to explain how all of these things have been prophesied in the Bible, and they will then begin preaching that these are the signs that the end of the world is near, so we may as well all just repent our sins and wait for the rapture.

Without question, this group of people has chosen to believe that we live in an unfriendly universe.

On the other hand, there are some people who believe just the opposite. Although they recognize that the previous point of view is valid in some respects, they choose to have a completely different interpretation of the same world events. These people recognize the fact that war exists, hatred exists, greed exists, poverty exists, and for the most part, human beings have a tendency to be afraid of one another, but they view the world from the perspective that the universe is perfect by design and is actually a very friendly place. They do not deny the so-called reality of the world; they simply have a different interpretation of what reality really is. They recognize that what appears to be total chaos is in fact divine creation in motion. They interpret the current world events from the metaphorical view of the transformation of the butterfly. From this perspective, they realize that in order for a caterpillar to be transformed into a butterfly, it must go through an amazing metamorphosis. So too must the Earth.

There is a story of a young boy who was watching a butterfly struggling to break free from his cocoon. As the boy watched the butterfly struggle, he felt a deep sense of sympathy for the butterfly's plight. In an attempt to help the butterfly, he decided that he would cut a small slit in the cocoon to make it easier for the butterfly to escape. It was with great joy that he watched the butterfly break free from his cocoon, but that joy turned to deep sadness as he watched the butterfly fall over, time and time again, and not be able to spread its wings and fly. After several minutes, he called his father to see if he had any suggestions to help the butterfly take flight. When he told his father what he had done, his father embraced him and told him the bad news. It turns out that the boy had actually condemned the butterfly to death by cutting the slit in the cocoon. His father explained to him that the butterfly's struggle in the cocoon was necessary to help it build the strength and endurance needed to fly. By cutting the slit and making it easier for it to escape, he had interrupted nature's way of preparing the butterfly for flight. Without the struggle, it could not and would not ever fly.

For those who believe that the universe is a friendly place, this story symbolizes the current transformational process that the world is currently experiencing. Their belief is that the world is currently going through a metamorphosis, and the current "negative" events of the world are simply the universe's way of preparing the world to eventually evolve into a world of love, peace, and understanding. Without this struggle, the world would not be able to become the beautiful, divine expression that it was created to be. In other words, without the struggle, humanity will never "fly." This group of people believes in the divine intelligence of the universe, and they accept the fact that flying is actually a part of our genetic makeup. They believe that all human beings are divine expressions of the universe, and encoded in their DNA is the blueprint for flight and for full self-expression. Like the butterfly, all people must go through their own personal struggles, which are mandatory for their growth and transformation. Without their struggles, they will never fly.

THE REVOLUTION

So the question you must now ask yourself is this, "Who's right?" Which of these two types of people is right? Is it the first group that believes in an unfriendly universe, or is it the second group that believes the universe is friendly?"

The fact of the matter is that they are both right. As Einstein said, we must decide whether or not we live in a friendly universe, and it is that decision that will ultimately shape our experience. You get to decide. So which do you choose, the belief in a friendly or unfriendly universe? The choice as always is yours.

I choose to believe in a friendly universe. Not only do I believe in a friendly universe, I also believe in my ability to assist the universe in transforming our world into becoming the beautiful expression that it is destined to become. Although I recognize all of the evidence to the contrary, I believe that we are currently moving into the most exciting and opportunistic times in the history of the planet.

Remember the quote from Steve Jobs in Chapter Three? Let me reprint it here to remind you. "The people who are crazy enough to think they can change the world, are the ones who do." As mentioned in an earlier chapter, I have always considered myself to be one of the crazy ones. My intention is to change the way men behave on this planet and to create a new paradigm of masculinity. But this is something that I can't do alone, so I would like to invite you to join me in my quest. I am now asking you to join my new revolution. This isn't a revolution of power, force, or control. It isn't an outer revolution but an inner revolution created to touch the minds, hearts, and souls of men. In this new revolution, men will embrace a new way of being men in today's ever-changing world.

As you're reading this, you may be inclined to think, "This guy is crazy." But that is a good thing. I'm inviting you to be crazy with me and to spread this new revolution around the globe.

So think about this for a moment. Was it crazy for Rosa Parks to refuse to give up her seat on that bus in 1955? Was it crazy for Martin Luther King Jr. to declare that he had a dream for America in which a man would be judged not by the color of his skin but by the content of his character? Was it crazy for Mahatma Gandhi to believe that he could use non-violent civil disobedience to free his country from British rule? Was it crazy for Nelson Mandela to believe that he could rid his country of apartheid and one day become its president? Did it make sense for these amazing visionaries to be bold enough, intelligent enough, courageous enough and definitely crazy enough to go against the status quo and trust their hearts in believing they could fulfill their dreams?

Of course not. When each of these amazing human beings began their revolutions, they were attacked, vilified, ridiculed, and even killed because the world could not see or understand their visions. But in the end, these amazing visionaries changed the course of human history and in the process made the world a better place.

My intention is not for you to risk your lives or become famous martyrs. In order to join this revolution, all you have to do is embrace a new conversation with men and make a commitment to adhering to the four cornerstones of an authentic man. If every man on this planet would embrace these cornerstones and become truly authentic men, then I believe we could create heaven right here on Earth. I've said it before, and I'll say it again, "Personal transformation leads to world transformation," and my goal is to transform the world one man at a time.

So let's recap the four cornerstones of an authentic male. The first cornerstone is FAITH. This means that a man develops an intimate relationship with the divine. He must choose the path that nurtures his soul, and he recognizes that there is a power greater than himself that he has direct access to. He commits to nurturing his relationship with the divine and uses spiritual principles in all of his interactions in life and with others.

The second cornerstone is ACCOUNTABILITY, which means that a man holds himself accountable for all of his actions and never places unjust blame on anyone else. He recognizes that his word is his bond and that his word is sacred and can be counted on no matter what.

The third cornerstone is INTEGRITY. This means a man does what's right even when he doesn't have to. It means living from a moral and spiritual code that aligns with his core values and principles. It means trusting his still, small voice within and letting it guide him through life. As a man of integrity, he knows what is expected of him, and his actions are always congruent with the principles of an authentic male.

The fourth cornerstone is RESPONSIBILITY. This means that a man takes complete responsibility for his emotional, intellectual, physical, and spiritual well-being. He takes the time to heal his heart and gains a deep understanding of who he is and why he is here. He recognizes that he must take complete responsibility for his life and success, and he knows that no one and nothing can stop him from living his dreams.

So are you up to the challenge? Are you committed to transforming yourself so that you can transform the world? Can you embrace the four cornerstones of an authentic male and incorporate them into your life? Can you align yourself with *A New Conversation with Men* and assist in creating a new paradigm of masculinity in the world?

If you can answer yes to these questions, congratulations! You are now an official ANCWM Revolutionary! As a revolutionary, it is your responsibility to follow the guidelines in this book and become the best man that you can be, so let's recap the contents to insure that you remember what you've learned.

In **Chapter One,** you learned how the conversation began. This chapter taught you that you must heed the words of Michael Jackson:

"If you wanna make the world a better place, Take a look at yourself, and then make a change."

In **Chapter Two,** you learned about our greatest challenge. It's important that you remember that our families, our cultures and the media shape our beliefs and perceptions of the world. As a result of this societal conditioning, we sometimes forget who we really are. Our greatest challenge is to know that all men have the capacity to be loving caring, nurturing, and supportive. We are not all angry, violent, and emotionally disconnected. The key is to recognize how our beliefs shape our realities, and if we want to experience something different in our lives, we must first be willing to change our beliefs.

In **Chapter Three,** you learned about the five illusions of manhood. They are:

To be a man, you must be non-emotional and disconnected. To be a man, you must have status, positions and power.

To be a man, you must have money and material possessions.

To be a man, you must use sexual conquest as a gauge for manhood. To be a man, you must win at all costs and compete against other men.

As a revolutionary, you are committed to waking up from these illusions and removing them from your consciousness.

Chapter Four taught you about the five masks of masculinity. They are:

Mr. Nice Guy

Mr. Tough as Nails

Mr. Money Bags

Mr. Gigolo

Mr. Stuck in His Head

As a revolutionary, you are committed to removing your masks and being an authentic male.

Chapter Five taught you about transformation. You learned the important lesson of going within, so you do not have to go without. You also learned that you must be willing to heal your own heart if you ever want to be able to be authentic and real with yourself.

Chapter Six taught you about the importance of creating and maintaining loving, caring, and monogamous relationships. You should have learned that being loved and loving someone are some of life's greatest pleasures. You should have also learned that it is possible to create a relationship (or marriage) that is rewarding and fulfilling.

Chapter Seven taught you about the importance of fatherhood and provided insights into becoming a better father. It pointed out that fatherlessness is one of society's greatest challenges, and it provided you with insights into becoming a better father.

Chapter Eight taught you about the importance of having joy in your life, and it encouraged you to express your creativity and to find your passions. This is the key to creating a meaningful and fulfilling life.

Chapter Nine encouraged you to examine your beliefs about God and to have a new conversation about the divine.

And here we are in **Chapter Ten** talking about your becoming a revolutionary. That means we have come full circle, and the teaching is complete. *A New Conversation with Men* should now be penetrating its way through your mind, heart, and spirit, and the transformation has begun.

Obviously, it's going to take a lot more than just reading this book to change the world, but I believe it's a great start. What has to happen now is that you take the lessons you have learned and apply them to your life. Use these lessons to make yourself a better man, and as you are transformed, so too is the world.

So I'd like to ask you to imagine this new, transformed world. In this new world, all men are loving, caring, compassionate, and authentic. Each man has replaced the love of power with the power of love, and there is peace and harmony on the planet. In this new world, no one goes to bed hungry and all children have the opportunity to reach their full potential. There are no wars and no prisons because there is no crime and no violence.

People from all religions have learned to be accepting of other people's beliefs without compromising their own, and interfaith churches and services are the norms, not the exception. People of all ethnicities embrace each other and recognize that differences do not necessarily mean that there have to be divisions. They can be different yet united, based on the understanding that we are all one anyway, no matter what your ethnicity or religion may be.

Can you imagine that world? Are you open to this possibility? Unfortunately, most people can't, but as an ANCWM revolutionary, you aren't like most people. You're one of the crazy ones, remember, so let's visualize this world together and watch it begin manifesting right away. Crazy people of the world, unite because the revolution has begun; it's time for *A New Conversation with Men!*

If you align with the contents of this book, I hope you will share it with others. All revolutions begin with crazy people and their dreams, and I am enrolling you in mine. I now declare that you are officially one of the crazy ones. Welcome! By sharing this book with others, the revolution will expand. Before you know it, men from all corners of the globe will unite, and this new conversation will replace the old paradigm of masculinity on the planet.

You can also stay connected by logging on to our website at www.anewconversationwithmen.com. The site is designed to be a resource for all men who align with this message and are committed to their own personal transformation. Log on and stay connected.

I'd like to take this opportunity to thank you for reading this book.

I sincerely appreciate the fact that not only were you courageous enough to read it, I honestly believe that if you have come this far in the book, then you are crazy enough to assist me in my vision. This really means a lot to me, and I wanted to thank you for participating. I'm really glad you have joined the revolution.

And now, it's time for me to say goodbye. I'm about to begin a new project that will insure that people keep calling me "crazy," so stay tuned for the next chapter of *A New Conversation with Men;* it's going to be a great one.

Peace!

About the author

Michael Taylor is an entrepreneur, author, motivational speaker and radio show host. He considers himself to be an irrepressible optimist with a passion for the impossible. He has dedicated his life to empowering men and women to become genuinely happy with their lives, and therefore, he writes books, facilitates lectures and provides a radio program dedicated to assisting men and women in this endeavor.

When he's not writing or lecturing, he enjoys, books, computers, movies, listening to 70's & 80's soul music, meditating and hanging out with his wife Bedra. He is happily married with three grown children and currently resides in Stafford, Texas which is a suburb located just south of Houston.

Books by the author:

Brother's Are You Listening? A Success Guide For The New Millennium

Black Men Rock

Adversity Is Your Greatest Ally

Lessons From A Gathering Of Men

Shattering Black Male Stereotypes

The New Face Of Entrepreneurship

The Cure For Onlyness

The Good News Is... The Future Is Brighter Than You Think

What If Jesus Were A Coach?

I'm Not Okay With Gray

The Brothahood Of Kings

Coach Michael Taylor websites

www.anewconversationwithmen.com

www.coachmichaeltaylor.com

www.shatteringblackmalestereotypes

www.jesuswasacoach.com

www.onlynesscure.com

www.joypassionprofit.com

www.brothahoodofkings.com

www.adversityisyourgreatestally.com

www.creationpublishing.com

www.ingramcontent.com/pod-product-compliance
Lightning Source LLC
Chambersburg PA
CBHW051427290426
44109CB00016B/1455